T0244462

A Moment in the Sun

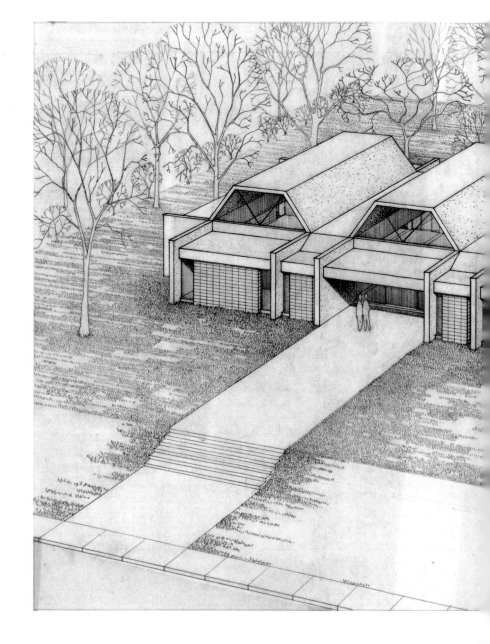

A Moment in the Sun:
Robert Ernest's Brief but
Brilliant Life in Architecture

ROBERT McCARTER

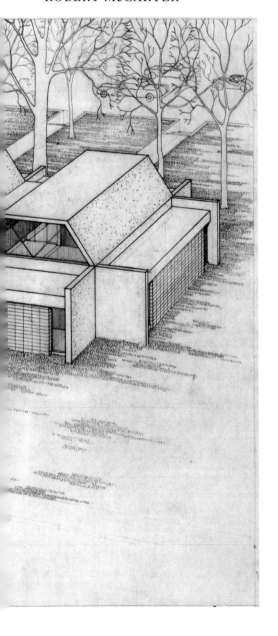

Novato, California

CONTENTS

Cover images:
Robert Ernest House, Atlantic Beach, Florida, 1960-61; exterior view.
Photograph by John W. Molitor.
Eli Becker House, Jacksonville, Florida, 1960-61; interior view. Photograph by Judith Gefter.

Page 2/3:
Municipal Youth Center, Jacksonville, Florida, 1961–62; final design,
presentation perspective, aerial view from northeast.

Fig. 1.1 Photograph of Robert Ernest.

Foreword

Robert Griffith Ernest (1933-62) was an architect of rare promise and remarkable early success, whose award-winning career was cut short by cancer at age twenty-eight in 1962. Despite the brevity of Ernest's life, his education and practice were intertwined with some of the most important figures in architecture, including his interactions with Louis I. Kahn during his post-graduate studies with Paul Rudolph at Yale University, and his working with Rudolph for two summers as well as supervising construction of Rudolph's last Florida house. Ernest's exceptional architectural designs, though honored during his lifetime with three *Progressive Architecture* Awards and one Record Houses Award, as well as being celebrated after his death in a solo exhibit at Yale University, and the dedication of *Perspecta 9/10* and an issue of the *Florida Architect* to his memory, have never been documented in a comprehensive manner and are now almost completely lost to disciplinary history.

Yet the materials in the architect's personal and professional archives covering the ten-year period from the beginning of his undergraduate education in 1952 until his death—on which this book is almost entirely based—clearly indicate that Ernest was a remarkably talented and unusually gifted architectural designer, whose future promise and potential were inestimable. Ernest's two built works, both realized before he turned twenty-eight, his one work built after his death, as well as the remarkably innovative unrealized projects documented in his archives, indicate that had Ernest lived to a normal lifespan, he would have been without question one of the most important architects of his generation, with the potential to design precedent-setting buildings equal to those realized by the most recognized architects in the sixty years after his death. This is evidenced by the fact that, while Ernest had only three buildings realized (one posthumously) during his brief two years as a sole practitioner in Jacksonville, Florida, these buildings have exercised a significant influence on more than one generation of Florida architects, as well as on the evolution of modern architecture in Florida after 1960.

Next pages:
Fig. 1.15 Sketch of Basilica, Vicenza, Italy, Andrea Palladio, 1957.
Fig. 1.2 Cartoon of caveman and Mondrian, ca. 1952–57.
Fig. 1.5 Cartoon of Christmas tree trimming, ca. 1952–57.

10/13/57

Undergraduate School, European Travel, and Internship 1933–1958

University of Virginia

Robert Griffith Ernest was born in Mobile, Alabama, on November 12, 1933. Ernest's family moved to Savannah, Georgia, and then to Jacksonville, Florida, where his father, Albert Ernest, was involved in the forestry products industry (fig. 1.1). Robert Ernest attended high school at the Bolles School for Boys, a private college-preparatory military school in the San José area of Jacksonville. Upon graduation from Bolles in 1951, he enrolled in the College of Arts and Sciences at the University of Virginia in Charlottesville, where he joined his older brother, Albert Jr., who was completing his second year. At the end of his first year of studies, on the recommendation of a friend, Martin Growald, a student in the School of Architecture, Robert Ernest enrolled in the five-year bachelor of architecture program at the University of Virginia in 1952.[1]

In addition to his skills in architectural design, while at University of Virginia Ernest was recognized for his talent as a sketch artist and cartoonist — in which he was inspired by the drawings of Saul Steinberg— by being appointed the cartoonist for the *Virginia Spectator*, the student journal. Ernest's cartoons are carefully composed for the maximum experiential effect with the minimum graphic effort, yet they also often have dense details that suggest deeper layers of meaning. His cartoons invariably exhibit the sense of humor for which Ernest was well-known, poking fun at conventions while still imparting the intended message.

 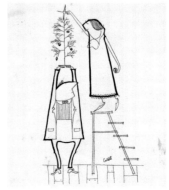

Examples include an animal skin-clad caveman carving a Mondrian-like composition on a cave wall (fig. 1.2); a large, sharp-pointed snowflake knocking the hat off a well-dressed gentleman (fig. 1.3); and an abstract rendition of a jazz trio of clarinet, bass, and piano, in which the linear outlines of the musicians' bodies fold inwards to become their arms, making a clever play of inside-outside and front-back (fig. 1.4). Many of the cartoons have a critical edge to them, either upending expectations, such as a bird in a birdcage whose enormously long beak is threatening a cat, and a couple in the movie theater where the woman reaches into the box in the man's lap and finds something more than popcorn, or poking provocatively at seasonal traditions, such as a woman on a ladder placing a star atop the small Christmas tree held high overhead by her husband (fig. 1.5) and a somewhat surly-looking, bell-ringing Santa Claus whose donation kettle has a child's leg sticking out of it.

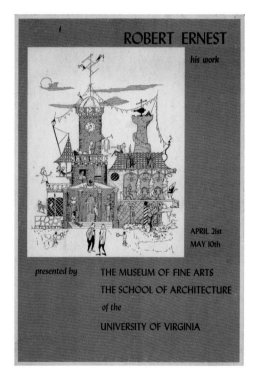

Fig. 1.6 Cartoon on poster for exhibition *Robert Ernest*, ca. 1952–57.

Fig. 1.7 Plan and section, ca. 1952–57; Villa Rotunda, Vicenza, Italy, Andrea Palladio.

Fig. 1.3 Cartoon of man and snowflake, ca. 1952–57.

Fig. 1.4 Cartoon of jazz trio, ca. 1952–57.

A MOMENT IN THE SUN

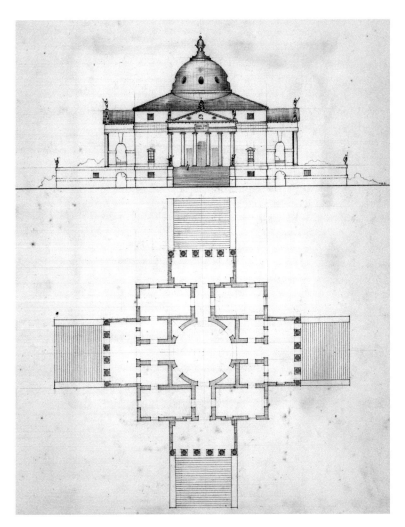

UNDERGRADUATE SCHOOL, EUROPEAN TRAVEL, AND INTERNSHIP

THE ADORATION OF THE MAGPI

Fig. 1.8 Drawing for Christmas card, ca. 1958–61.

During his time as a student at the University of Virginia, the University Museum of Fine Arts and the School of Architecture held a joint exhibit of his cartoons and sketches. The cartoon Ernest designed for the exhibit, included on the poster, depicts his humorous take on undergraduate college life, with all manner of mishaps and misbehaviors taking place in an architectural setting. The cartoon presents a wildly eclectic fraternity house composed of a pedimented tower surrounded by unmatched pavilions where a party is in full swing, with broken windows, errant ping pong and billiard balls, formal diners at table, and trombone players on the roof. Naked female caryatids support the arcade, which has wildly mismatched architectural columns (fig. 1.6).[2] The cartoon may also be interpreted as a humorous if somewhat scandalous view of the degradation resulting from student inhabitation of Thomas Jefferson's buildings on the Lawn at the University of Virginia, where undergraduate dorm rooms line the lower colonnade and faculty "houses" form the upper colonnade.

The cartoons also reveal Ernest's considerable skills at delineation, both in terms of accurately recording a scene or subject with minimal linework and in capturing the character of a place or event with an eye for the most compelling composition. The carefully drawn elevations and plans of Palladian villas, including the Villa Rotunda in Vicenza, Italy (fig. 1.7), part of a research paper on Palladio for a history class, show that Ernest had a command of the graphite and pencil medium equal to that of the ink and pen he used in his cartoons and travel sketches. Throughout his life, his many sketches—for travel, architectural design, or pleasure—would be characterized by exceptional clarity, rigor, and simplicity. His continuing interest in cartoons is reflected in the Christmas card he made several years later, in which the three wise men or magi are depicted as birds bearing gifts for a baby bird in a nest beneath a gold star, titled "The Adoration of the Magpi" (fig. 1.8).

After a somewhat bumpy start, Ernest's grades slowly improved during his five years in architecture school, with C's in architectural design studio in his second year (but with an A in the model-making course), B's in his third year, and A's in his fourth year. Intriguingly, given his masterful deployment of structure and concrete in his later career, Ernest was consistently given C grades in the architectural engineering and statics courses, as well as in the reinforced concrete design course during his fourth year. However, perhaps in an indication of the "grade inflation" that has occurred at universities since that time, these C's did not keep Ernest from making the Dean's List in spring 1955, fall 1955, and spring 1956.[3]

In the summer of 1954, following his second year in architecture school, Ernest, then aged twenty, married Lynwood Ingerville Evans, whom he had met during his high school years in Jacksonville, where she attended the Bartram School for Girls. They spent their honeymoon at an art school in Banff in Alberta, Canada, where Ernest took classes in painting for credits that were transferred to the University of Virginia. After the wedding, Lynwood transferred from Florida State University in Tallahassee to University of Virginia. The couple's daughter Kim was born in Charlottesville in 1956.

In the summer of 1955, following Ernest's third year in the architecture program, he was offered a two-month internship working directly with Paul Rudolph in his small satellite office in Cambridge, Massachusetts (his main office was located in Sarasota, Florida). This remarkable opportunity to work directly with one of the most widely recognized architects in the United States and the leading member of the important regional group of modern architects, later called the "Sarasota School," would quite literally change Ernest's life. The projects that were in Rudolph's Cambridge office that summer included the US Embassy in Amman, Jordan, the additions to the Sarasota High School in Sarasota, Florida, and the Jewett Arts Center at Wellesley College in Wellesley, Massachusetts. Ernest would also have been interested in the projects that were in Rudolph's Sarasota office, with which Rudolph was in constant contact throughout the summer. These included the Stinnett Residence in Sarasota, a single-story, modular wood-frame house elevated off the ground and surrounded by a loggia equipped with pivoting wooden panels that when opened provided shade and when closed protected against hurricane winds. Also on the boards was the Biggs Residence in Delray Beach, a single-story pavilion-like house elevated one floor off the ground on a steel frame, forming an open-air living space beneath the house, with the main floor of the house arranged around an open central living room, and the north and south walls of the house entirely opened with operable jalousie windows. While it is not clear which projects the inexperienced Ernest worked on while in Rudolph's Cambridge office in 1955, his work and skills were of sufficient quality that Ernest was hired to work as an intern in Rudolph's Sarasota office the next summer.[4]

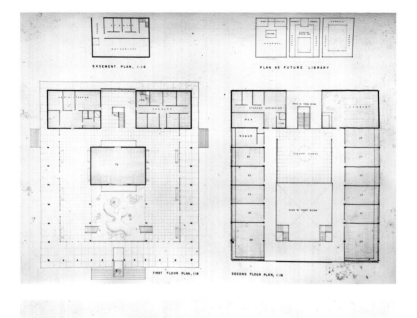

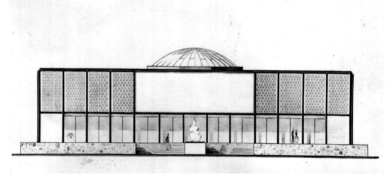

Fig. 1.9 Clinch Valley College, University of Virginia project, 1956; floorplans.
Fig. 1.10 Clinch Valley College, front elevation.

In the spring of 1956, during his fourth year in the architecture program, Ernest's design for Clinch Valley College, the first building of a
new extension college of the University of Virginia, was awarded first
prize in a five-week competition.[5] The three-story building would initially
be used for all aspects of the new college, later becoming the central
library of the new campus (figs. 1.9 and 1.10). Ernest's design proposed
a near-square plan of two floors with a largely open lower floor resting
on a raised stone-walled plinth, opened to the east, south, and west with
full-height glazed walls set back behind a colonnade of steel perimeter
columns, solid-walled blocks of administrative and faculty offices to the
north, and a free-standing auditorium sharing the center with a garden
court set beneath a low spherical glass dome. A central stair in the double-height space between the two solid-walled blocks to the north and a
pair of stairs rising at the southern corner of the garden court, together
gave access to the second floor, a U-shape plan opening to the south with
a library, offices, and services in the solid blocks to the north and classrooms along the east and west wings, accessed from the walkway running
around the student lounge (above the auditorium) and overlooking the
garden court.

Ernest's design, with its rectangular, largely glass-walled volume
framed by the exposed structural columns and beams (including the corners and the top and bottom of its solid-walled northern facade), was
clearly influenced by Mies van der Rohe's contemporary designs for the
Illinois Institute of Technology (IIT) campus in Chicago, under construction from 1943 to 1956, one of the most influential modern university campuses in the world. Less Miesian are the vertical, offset-pattern
metal sun-shading screens attached to the second-floor glass walls on
the east, south, and west sides, which are reminiscent of contemporary
designs such as Paul Rudolph's Jewett Arts Center at Wellesley College,
drawings for which Ernest would have seen while working in Rudolph's
Sarasota office the summer before, as well as the low, radially ribbed
glass dome over the central garden court, which is similar to Frank Lloyd
Wright's dome at the top of the Guggenheim Museum in New York, then
beginning construction.

In the summer of 1956, Ernest was employed in the Sarasota office of
Paul Rudolph, where he worked under the direction of Rudolph's associate, Bert Brosmith. Letters from Rudolph to Brosmith refer to Ernest having been hired, with Rudolph telling Brosmith, "you will have to closely
direct his work for the only experience he has had was two months with
me last summer," as well as to Ernest's work on at least two projects.
Rudolph specifically refers to Ernest's work on the Burkhardt Residence
on Casey Key, telling Brosmith, "the last plans you sent on Burkhardt
were not thought out at all. I assume Bob [Ernest] did them. You will
have to show him specifically what to do."[6] The Burkhardt Residence is

a masterful reinterpretation of Frank Lloyd Wright's contemporary Usonian houses, its wood-framed glass exterior walls, concrete block interior walls, and extensive flat roof overhangs on all sides creating an atmosphere redolent of the Japanese inspiration for Wright's Prairie houses, especially in the markedly Japanese character of its post-and-beam wood frame. The other house on which Ernest worked that summer was Rudolph's Deering Residence on Casey Key, with its L-shaped plan wrapping around a double-height, screened porch facing the ocean, its regular rhythm of vertical concrete piers, its massive parallel concrete block walls, and its multilevel living room stepping majestically down towards the beach. The Deering Residence exemplifies the change in Rudolph's work taking place at this time, from the earlier quality of attenuated lightness, realized in wood and steel construction, to the later quality of heavier, more monumental character, constructed in reinforced concrete and concrete block, which also served to connect Rudolph's works to the contemporary designs of Louis Kahn.

Ernest's final or thesis project of 1956–57, involving a self-determined design program, was for the renovation of Fort Adams of 1812, set between Narragansett Bay and the Atlantic Ocean in Newport, Rhode Island, to house the Newport Jazz Festival. Ernest worked from a program of spaces provided by the Jazz Festival organizers, and as a result his academic design was seriously considered for implementation at Fort Adams, though in the end it did not go forward. In a way strikingly different from his proposals for new buildings, such as the Clinch Valley College competition, Ernest's thesis design was remarkably respectful of the existing historical ruins, being formally reserved and proposing to add only aerial, lightweight fabric structures that would complement, rather than compete with, the massive, earth-bound masonry of the fort.

Ernest's design was presented in rendered plans and sections, a detailed model showing the fort and its surroundings, and eye-level perspective ink sketches (figs. 1.11 and 1.12). Ernest proposed that the major Jazz Festival performances would take place in an amphitheater sited in and gently excavated from the most enclosed corner of the central courtyard, and that the new amphitheater would be covered with a large hexagonal fabric canopy supported by tension cables strung between a single column that rose through an opening at the center and six peripheral columns. This was the first of what would be numerous uses of hexagonal roof canopy structures in Ernest's work. Ernest proposed that the existing cell-like rooms that are built into the thickness of the outer wall and ring the courtyard of Fort Adams would be repurposed as practice rooms for the musicians, administration, private dining rooms, and exhibition spaces. These rooms would be connected at the rear by aligned doorways, and each would be given a canopy that provides cover both above the door facing the courtyard and over the seating space on the grass-covered

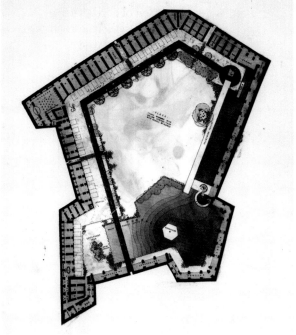

Fig. 1.11 Thesis project, Fort Adams Jazz Festival, University of Virginia project, 1956–57; aerial view of model.
Fig. 1.12 Fort Adams Jazz Festival, floorplan.

UNDERGRADUATE SCHOOL, EUROPEAN TRAVEL, AND INTERNSHIP

Fig. 1.13 Sketch of walls of Carcassonne, France, 1957.

Fig. 1.14 Sketch of Palazzo Vecchio, Florence, Italy, 1957.

roof above. The courtyard itself would be paved with hexagonal concrete pavers with circular central openings that could be filled with gravel to allow rain to percolate or filled with earth to allow grass to grow.

After graduating from the University of Virginia in the spring of 1957, Ernest studied for two months at the architecture school at Fontainebleau, France—making a very precise ink sketch of a detail of the chateau—after which he traveled for five more months throughout Europe. As documented in his characteristically detailed sketches, Ernest spent time in Italy, including Venice, Vicenza, Verona, Florence, and Milan, as well as Barcelona in Spain and Carcassonne in France (fig. 1.13), where he drew the towers of the walled city from the same vantage point that Louis Kahn would take when he visited two years later. In the largely ink sketches, Ernest was able to capture the essential aspects of a building or place with a few lines and carefully crafted detail. Examples include the remarkable one-inch-square sketch of the Palazzo Vecchio and its tower in Florence (fig. 1.14), the sketches of Piazza San Marco, the Ca' d'Oro, and Palladio's San Giorgio Maggiore in Venice, the sketch of the corner of Palladio's Basilica in Vicenza (fig.1.15), and the sketch of the courtyard of San Ambrogio in Milan—all of which measure less than four inches on a side.

Ernest also spent considerable time in Athens and the Greek islands, where he took many black-and-white photographs of the white-washed buildings that seem to grow from the terraced hillsides. His pencil-and-ink sketches of the rounded forms of the Greek Orthodox churches were later reworked into simple vignettes, and some of his photographs and his inked figure-ground plan of the town of Mykonos were included in an article entitled "Mykonos and Patmos," which he coauthored with the

Yale third-year studio critic Paul Mitarachi, and which was published in 1960 in *Perspecta* 6, the journal of the Yale University Architecture School. While the 1959 article was the direct result of Mitarachi's recent travels made possible by the Wheelwright Traveling Fellowship he received upon graduating from Harvard, it also drew on Ernest's 1957 travels and included the photographs and sketches of both authors.

Mitarachi and Ernest's article makes an argument for a reintegration of history and so-called popular building into modern architecture and compares the two Greek settlements to reveal the nuances of place as well as "the proper balance between the individual parts and the harmonious whole." The article compares and contrasts the subtle differences between the relatively flat island and town of Mykonos, with its all-white-washed, "adobe-like," curved-edged residential buildings and 360 chapels for 3,500 inhabitants, the former exclusively flat-roofed, while pitched roofs are reserved for the chapels that punctuate almost every one of the pedestrian streets, and on the island of Patmos, the hilltowns of Chora, built around the eleventh-century monastery, and Scala, where the sharp-edged, white-washed walls of both town's buildings are opened with rectangular, stone-framed windows and doors. "The contrast between the sharp self-contained cubes of Patmos and the fluidity of [the house-forms of] Mykonos is striking." Despite their formal and urban differences, the two towns employ the same construction methods, and in both towns "individualism is expressed within the measure of an almost intangible harmony which, however, never becomes uniformity."[7]

When published in *Perspecta* 6, the Mitarachi and Ernest article was framed by "The Observatories of the Maharajah Sawai Jai Singh II" at Delhi and Jaipur, India, a photographic essay by the Japanese-American sculptor Isamu Noguchi that was to influence the American architect Louis I. Kahn, and "'The Functional Tradition' and Expression" by British architect James Stirling, in which he draws parallels between his own designs and vernacular and historic British buildings. The journal also included essays on Machu Picchu by Yale historian Vincent Scully and Hadrian's Villa by UC Berkeley professor Charles Moore, later dean of Yale, and the whole reflects the renewed interest in reintegrating disciplinary history into architectural education and practice that characterized the years Ernest was in graduate school at Yale (1958–59).

Fig. 1.16 Convent, New Orleans, BLL Architects, 1958; ground-floor plan (left), upper-floor plan (right), section (above right).

Internship at Burk, LeBreton, and Lamantia, Architects, New Orleans, Louisiana

In December 1957 Ernest returned to the United States and moved to New Orleans, Louisiana, where he worked as a designer for Burk, LeBreton, and Lamantia, Architects, a firm headed by William Burk, Denvrich LeBreton, and James Lamantia that was then engaged in designing a variety of public, university, and religious buildings in New Orleans and the surrounding region. During his less than nine months with the firm, the twenty-four-year-old Ernest was involved in designing several remarkably resolved projects and buildings, which are documented in his portfolio, where what would be the typical characteristics of his later academic and professional designs can already be discerned. In this period, he also sat for the exam and received his license to practice architecture.

Ernest's design for a small convent organizes the program on two floors, with collective spaces on the lower floor and private spaces on the upper level, both of which are centered on a double-height stair hall illuminated and passively cooled (by chimney effect) by a clerestory window-banded cupola at the top (figs. 1.16 and 1.17). On the main lower floor, the entry from the south is visually separated from the central stair hall by a vertical wood slat screen. The entry foyer is flanked on either side by a pair of parlors for receiving visitors, their northern walls solid so as not to compromise the privacy of the sisters' monastic life within.

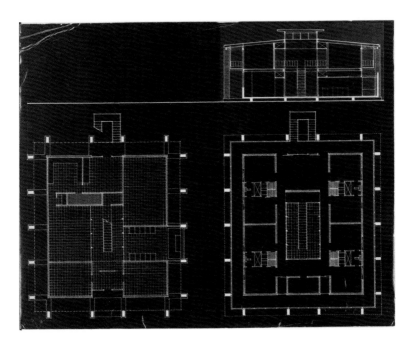

Fig. 1.17 Convent; model.

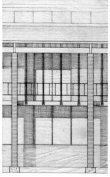

Fig. 1.18 Convent, elevation detail study of one structural bay.

The large dining room on the west side opens through a full-height glass wall to the central hall. Across the hall is the full-height glass wall of the chapel, where the sisters sit facing each other on the solid north and south walls, with the raised chancel, altar, and apse projecting out to the east to receive light from north and south and above, as well as through the high clerestory window opening to the east, but also to maintain privacy. The sisters' community room, the largest space in the convent, is placed in the northeast corner. The kitchen, laundry, and mechanical are placed in the northwest corner, with a second stair projecting to the north on the exterior. On the upper floor, eight cells are set in four pairs sharing bathrooms, with a sewing room to the north and entry to the cells from the narrow hall around the central stair hall, with a broad balcony ringing the outside of the building.

The brick structural piers run around the building perimeter and rise the full height of the building (fig. 1.18). In plan, the piers frame four twelve-foot-wide bays running east-west and two larger sixteen-foot-wide bays set to the east and west of the twelve-foot-wide central bay, running north-south. The piers are placed well outside the building's exterior walls on extended foundations and are set back to form reentrant corners. The piers stand on the upstanding foundation beams supporting the raised lower floor, and the piers carry the upper floor beams extending out beneath the balcony and the low-hipped roof structure, which bears directly on top of the piers. The interior ceilings are lowered to door-top height along the east and west edges of the central hall on both floors, accommodating the air conditioning ducts and creating a lower transition zone between the higher ceilings of the rooms and the central hall. In addition to the chimney-effect cooling provided by the central stair hall, the interior climate is also tempered by the continuous upper-level balcony and broad overhang of the hipped roof, which shade

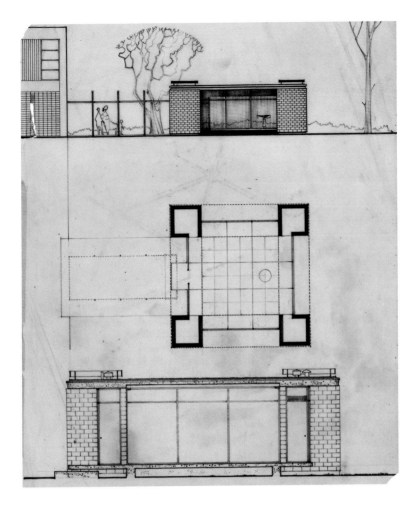

Fig. 1.19 Baptistry, New Orleans, BLL Architects, 1958; plan and section (below), elevation (above).

Fig. 1.20
One Engine
Fire Station, New Orleans,
BLL Architects, 1958;
exterior perspective.

UNDERGRADUATE SCHOOL, EUROPEAN TRAVEL, AND INTERNSHIP

the windows of the deeply recessed outer walls of both floors. The carefully proportioned elevation study and the models of the building indicate that it would have provided the sisters a shaded, private retreat that was open to breezes, light, and views.

A small baptistry, designed by Ernest as a free-standing addition to an existing church, has a square plan with solid corners and open centers (fig. 1.19). Four concrete block–walled hollow piers anchor the corners and contain the services, with all-glass walls facing the cardinal directions recessed behind the shading overhangs of the thin concrete roof and standing on recessed and cantilevered concrete floor slabs, with deep shadows beneath. The entry is from the west, passing beneath a canopy framed with thin steel posts the same dimensions as the window mullions within the baptistry, stepping up onto the large threshold slab that rises from the ground and then stepping up onto the cantilevered floor of the baptistry. Inside, the cylindrical baptismal font is placed on the east side, and the square, central space of ritual is subtly emphasized by the slight elevation of the ceiling height, its four outer edges illuminated by linear bands of up lights. For those standing within the baptistry, with views opening outwards in the four cardinal directions, the overhanging roof, thicker at its outer edge, creates a deep shadow, with the floor and glazing recessed within, and the memory of seeing the deep shadow beneath the raised floor slab confirms the levitation of the entire room above the ground. The baptistry design is a variation on the ancient theme of square and cruciform plans for centralized churches, with solid, closed corner towers framing projecting, open central volumes, extending from the Renaissance to Frank Lloyd's Wright's Unity Temple of 1906. One is reminded of Ernest's university drawings of the plan and elevation of Palladio's Villa Rotunda, which similarly opens from its central room in four directions and is framed by four solid corner blocks.

A single perspective drawing, rendered in Ernest's distinctive manner, presents a one-engine fire station that proudly displays the bright red fire engine in its glass-walled vitrine-like room (fig. 1.20). A steel-frame of thin columns and beams, five smaller bays on the long sides and a single large bay on the short sides, supports a flat roof and stands on a concrete slab on grade. The entirely glass-walled enclosure for the engine is recessed within the larger outer frame and roof, and the gravel driveway penetrates from outside into the center of the U-shaped concrete floor slab. A smaller solid-walled, two-story volume is set at the back, and contains the working spaces on the ground floor and the crew room on the upper level, accessed by stairs behind the end wall of the engine room. The upper level is wrapped on the three outer walls by high, horizontal clerestory windows formed by the glazed wall surrounding the larger engine space. While the vitrine-like display of the fire engine suggests that the fire station is also a museum, the detailing of the minimal steel

Fig. 1.22
High School Gymnasium;
model.

frame may be related to the domestic works of Mies van der Rohe, such as the Farnsworth House of 1950, or Philip Johnson's own Glass House of 1949, where domestic life is displayed as if on exhibit.

Ernest's design for the gymnasium addition to the De La Salle High School, which had been built to the designs of Burk, LeBreton, and Lamantia in 1950, was set to the south of the existing high school buildings (fig. 1.21). The large gymnasium has three levels: a large, covered sports and entry space at the ground; the main, triple-height, column-free gymnasium elevated to the first floor, with banks of seating along the east and west sides; and a large sports terrace on the roof. Three pairs of massive, solid-walled masonry towers containing stairs, structure, and services frame the north and south sides of the building, accessed from the passages on either side of the ground-floor sports space, and the roof terrace is supported by the deep-truss structure spanning from north to south between the towers. The angled blocks of stepped seating projecting to the east and west are supported at their outer edges by a series of steel piers carrying diagonal bracing and rising to support butterfly canopy roofs at the edges of the roof terrace. A model photograph likely shows a later variation on the east and west ends, where the space beneath the stepped seating is partly enclosed to provide a series of small sports courts, illuminated by the continuous, large clerestory windows above (fig. 1.22). As with many of Ernest's models, scale figures, sometimes cut from photographs in magazines and sometimes drawn, are deployed throughout to illustrate the human scale of the spaces. Though the gymnasium was realized to a different design, without the open space beneath, the sports terrace on the roof, or the functionally shaped interior volumes expressed on the exterior, the clarity with which the various enclosed volumes and the structure are articulated in Ernest's proposal will prove typical of his designs.[8]

During this period in New Orleans, Ernest prepared an independent project for a studio and minimal dwelling for the musician James G. Roy Jr. in the San José neighborhood of Jacksonville. Roy had been Ernest's high school music teacher at the nearby Bolles School, and the program for the minimal dwelling-studio called for one large room with space for

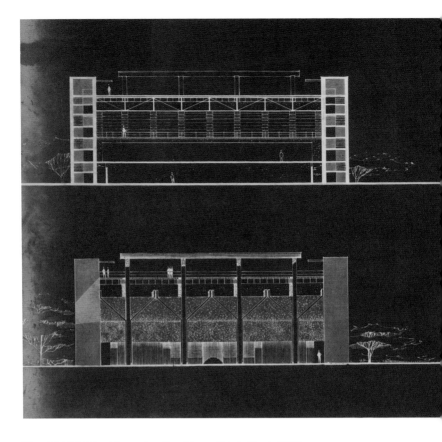

Fig. 1.21 High School Gymnasium, New Orleans, BLL Architects, 1958; elevations (below), sections (above).

two pianos and storage for 10,000 records. Ernest's design proposed a rectangular, twenty-by-thirty-two-foot floor plan divided into five eight-by-twenty-foot bays with eight-foot-tall solid walls on all four sides (fig. 1.23). The entry door is in the center of the one of the twenty-foot walls, and the kitchen window in the center of the other twenty-foot wall is the only eye-level aperture. Continuous record shelving is placed along the two thirty-two-foot walls, and the bath, small kitchen, closet, desk, and bed are placed against the twenty-foot wall opposite the entry, concealed by a projecting solid-walled, U-shaped-in-plan volume that provides a backdrop for the two pianos—a grand piano and a vertical piano.

The building is structured by five pairs of wood columns, set at eight-foot centers along the thirty-two-foot sidewalls, and the elevated floor and ceiling are supported by pairs of wood beams, spaced apart by being attached to the sides of the columns, and spanning the twenty-foot width of the room (fig. 1.24). Four eight-by-twenty-foot plywood barrel

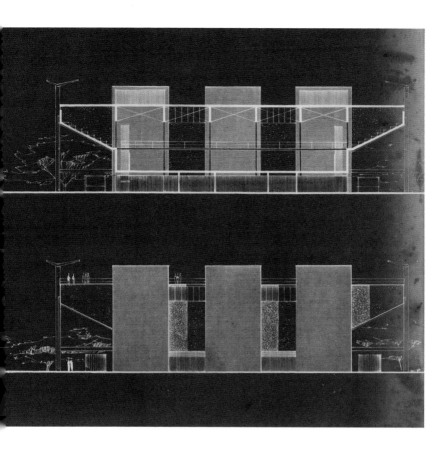

vaults, which bear on the upper pairs of wood beams and span the room, form the ceiling and roof. In his portfolio, Ernest states that the plywood vaults are "tie-rodded" to resist outward thrust, but the tie-rods or cables are not shown in the perspectives or drawings. The curving ends of the vaults are glazed, divided into three sections by vertical mullions, providing the only daylight and views outwards from within the room. This design indicates Ernest's familiarity with the use of plywood roof vaults, pioneered by Sarasota architect Paul Rudolph, first proposed in 1951 in his Hook Guest House and first realized in 1953 in his Sanderling Beach Club, both on Florida's Siesta Key.

Ernest's interior perspective, looking from near the entry towards the pianos at the other end, has its eye level located near the floor, and thus emphasizes the space- and sound-shaping qualities of the vaulted ceiling in the intended experience of the room (fig. 1.25). The simple elegance of the pavilion, the elevated floor, and the strict symmetry of the plan, elevations, and entry sequence—with the pianos set in the apse-like space opposite the front door, where the altar would be in a chapel—together indicate Ernest's deeply spiritual interpretation of this dwelling. Ernest's carefully detailed elevation studies, with his client pictured standing at the raised threshold of the front door, show the shadows of the projecting pairs of beams at the floor and ceiling and indicate the vertical-board siding of the wall beneath the glazed vaults was to be framed by the wooden columns to either side and by fascia trim boards on the top and bottom. The entry elevation, with two perfect squares of framed, vertical-board siding set on either side of the entry door, the floor and ceiling beams projecting to either side, and the roof vault curving away above, suggests one is about to enter a formalized, temple-like pavilion for a Shinto tea ceremony or similar ritual, again emphasizing the intensely spiritual quality Ernest intended for the room of sound within.

Fig. 1.24 Roy Studio; side elevation.

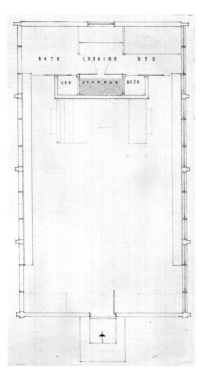

Fig. 1.23
Roy Studio, Jacksonville, 1958;
floorplan.

Fig. 1.25 Roy Studio; interior perspective.

UNDERGRADUATE SCHOOL, EUROPEAN TRAVEL, AND INTERNSHIP

Graduate School
and Apprenticeship
1958–1960

Yale University, Master Class with Paul Rudolph

From September 1958 to June 1959, Ernest was one of nineteen graduate students in the Master Class, the one-year, post-professional master of architecture program at Yale University intended for students already possessing a professional bachelor of architecture degree. At that time the faculty included the remarkably influential historians George Kubler, William MacDonald, Frank Brown, and Vincent Scully. Their collective teaching and writings reflected the renewed efforts during this time to integrate disciplinary history into architectural education and practice, which stood in contrast to the efforts to remove history from the curriculum at other modern schools such as the Graduate School of Design at Harvard University, where Walter Gropius, founder of the Bauhaus, headed the architecture program from 1937-52.

Perhaps the most influential historian at Yale, in terms of his impact on the architecture students, was George Kubler, whose unprecedented interpretation of art and architectural history, as recorded in pre-Columbian artworks and architectural spaces, was published in the 1962 book entitled *The Shape of Time*. Kubler held that works of art and architecture from the past "are still open to further elaboration by new solutions," and he proposed an all-encompassing understanding of works of art and architecture as belonging to the history of things as forms that are continuously evolving through time. According to Kubler, history understood as the shape of time engaged with all human-made things, from crafts to architecture to art, as variations on themes in a continuously linked evolution of forms across time: "Today it is again apparent that the artist is an artisan, that he belongs to a distinct human grouping as *homo faber*, whose calling is to evoke a perpetual renewal of form in matter." Regarding the relation of materials to making, Kubler held that the artist-craftsman "was bound to achieve his unconventional aim with conventional means," suggesting that works of the highest quality need not be made from the rarest or most expensive materials.[9]

William MacDonald was studying and documenting Roman vaulting techniques more comprehensively than had been done before, and he was also investigating the employment of Roman techniques in the Romanesque and Byzantine periods,[10] and in his lectures and writings he emphasized the interior space-making capacity of the brick- and-concrete structural masses of the walls and vaulted ceilings of Roman architecture, as experienced from within. Frank Brown was already internationally recognized as an authority on ancient Rome,[11] and Brown would guide generations of architects on tours of the Roman ruins during the time he was resident archaeologist of the American Academy in Rome. Last but by no means least, the young Vincent Scully's inspiring lectures examining the Greek sites and the Roman spaces effectively reestablished these ancient cultures as relevant to the education of modern architects.[12] Scully's teaching also increasingly focused on North American modern architecture, and even more precisely on the work of Frank Lloyd Wright. Scully's intense examination of Wright's entire body of work, and his enthusiastic descriptions of the experience of space in Wright's buildings, had a powerful effect on the architecture students.[13]

Also on the faculty was the artist and educator Josef Albers, who chaired the Department of Design and taught the basic design course to both art and architecture students, based on the similar course he taught first at the Bauhaus and later at Black Mountain College. While it is not clear that Ernest was enrolled in Albers's course, which was only required for the undergraduate students, Albers's teaching permeated the school so completely during this time that Ernest was certain to have been aware of and likely influenced by it. Albers stated that in all art, which for him included architecture, "precision – as to the effect wanted – and discipline – as to the means used—are decisive", and he emphasized the experienced qualities of each *material*—texture, color, depth, hardness—and the way it received and returned sunlight.[14]

In a 1944 essay, Albers argued that architecture students should be educated in what was, after all, still the "handmade" craft of building, to experience the qualities of the materials with which they built, and to reveal in the finished building the process of its construction.[15] In his teaching, Albers had his students first draw a wide variety of materials, attempting to capture the subtle differences in texture and color, and then employ those same materials in collage-like compositions intended to highlight each material's inherent character. According to Albers, the primary intention of these exercises was to "develop understanding of and respect for material,"[16] which for Ernest would have paralleled and reinforced Kubler's findings in *The Shape of Time*.

Complementing the teaching of the full-time faculty, the visiting studio faculty during Ernest's time at Yale included a number of renowned practitioners such as Ludwig Mies van der Rohe, head of the IIT School of Architecture, and James Stirling, then emerging as the most important British architect of his generation, who emphasized the engagement of the historical and cultural contexts of buildings, as well as the history of modern architecture. The Philadelphia architect Louis I. Kahn, who had been the chief critic in architecture at Yale since 1950, and in recent years the critic for the Master Class, was at this time completing his transition from Yale to the University of Pennsylvania. Kahn's departure was least partly the result of Paul Rudolph having been appointed chair of architecture at Yale in the spring of 1958. Upon arriving at Yale, Rudolph took over the Master Class, which doubled in size from the previous year, and Ernest, who had worked for two summers in Rudolph's Cambridge and Sarasota offices, was among the first students to enroll.

Ernest had some contact with Kahn, who still exercised considerable influence on the architecture program at Yale, and it is critically important to note that Ernest's studio classes took place on the top floor of Kahn's 1953 Yale Art Gallery, beneath the powerful tetrahedral concrete ceiling structure where Kahn had taught the Master Class studios until 1957. This was the first building where Kahn endeavored to expose all the materials of construction, inside and out, exactly as they had emerged from the process of construction, including the cast concrete structural ceiling and piers, the wall infill materials of concrete block, brick, and glazing, and exhibiting rather than covering the marks of the process of making, as exemplified in the wood board–form marks and tie holes in the cast concrete walls and piers. This frank expression of the materials of making, including the extensive use of concrete block on the interior walls, would have a profound effect on Ernest. Late in his life Kahn would confirm the importance of the lessons that can only be drawn from inhabiting a building, and he would conclude that, though he was a teacher of architecture all his life, the only true lessons one architect can give another are those embodied in their buildings: "And so it is, when a work is done, that the work actually teaches tremendously. It teaches by example, or rather I would say by deed, and that, of course, is the powerful force of Le Corbusier, Frank Lloyd Wright, and Michelangelo. . . . They did not teach in a school. They taught by their work."[17]

Both Kahn and Rudolph often assigned their own current professional office projects as studio programs, so that the Yale students were made aware of two architects' most recent designs and their evolution. While Rudolph directed the Master Class during Ernest's time at Yale, Kahn's influence remained strong, and Rudolph encouraged his students that had an interest in Kahn to visit him in Philadelphia. It is worth noting that three years later, in 1961–62, when Norman Foster and Richard Rogers were graduate students in Rudolph's Master Class, their team design for the Pierson-Sage Science Complex on the Yale campus of 1961 was inspired not by Rudolph's work but by Kahn's Richards Medical Laboratory towers at the University of Pennsylvania, which were in construction at the time Ernest was at Yale. Ernest undertook at least five design projects, and possibly a sixth, while in the nine-month master of architecture program at Yale, and they are all of a remarkably high quality.

Rudolph began the Master Class with a one-week sketch project for a large high school, based on the programs for two high schools he was then building in Sarasota, Florida.[18] Ernest's design, which is similar in several ways to his award-winning fourth year undergraduate design for the Clinch Valley College, has a rectangular, golden section-proportioned, two-story plan, elongated in the east-west direction (figs. 2.1 and 2.2). A square courtyard, around which the double-height entry with large circular skylights, classrooms, and library are gathered, centers the larger eastern section of the school. The western section of the school, with the cafeteria, kitchen, and loading below the gymnasium and auditorium above, and classrooms flanking the north and south sides, is joined to the eastern section of the school by a longitudinal court. The central block of the western section of the school, housing the large shared rooms, is covered by a folded plate concrete roof, opened by linear skylights, which spans from large piers set along the east and west edges—similar to Kahn's design for the Trenton Jewish Community Center gymnasium that same year (fig. 2.3). The hallways leading to the second-floor classrooms are top lit by pyramidal skylights, and projecting sunscreens protect the facades of all the classrooms (fig. 2.4). The sunscreens are composed of circular forms touching at the edges (similar to the paving pattern of the courtyard) and are supported by tapered steel columns that are largest at the center and smallest at the the top (roof) and bottom (ground). The double-height entry foyer is recessed behind four tapered columns and its five bays are each opened with a large circular, domed skylight. The windows of the library open onto the entry foyer at the second floor.

Similar "handshake" projects, intended to give the faculty an immediate reading of the capacities of the new students, while not uncommon at the start of post-professional architecture programs, usually have smaller and simpler programs than those Rudolph gave to Ernest and his fellow students. For example, when teaching at Yale as a visiting critic in 1955, Rudolph gave the program for a Tastee-Freez ice cream stand as the one-week opening project—a choice that was criticized by many of the other Yale faculty, including Kahn, for not being an institutional program. Rudolph later noted that the large high school program he had given Ernest and his fellow Master Class students involved "a year's worth of work,"[19] yet Ernest's design for this one-week sketch project is remarkably resolved. When placed under such pressure to perform, it is not surprising that Ernest fell back to some extent on his undergraduate Clinch Valley College design, but his design for his first Yale project was less inspired by Mies van der Rohe and instead more closely related to contemporary designs by Edward Durell Stone, Kahn, and Rudolph.

With the exception of the first project and his final thesis, the order in which Ernest undertook the other three (or four) Yale projects is not indicated in his portfolio. The design for an underground restaurant

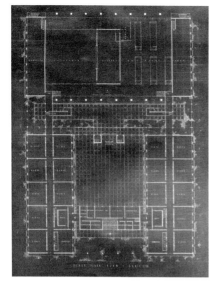

Fig. 2.1 High School, Yale project, 1958; first-floor plan.

Fig. 2.2 High School; second-floor plan.

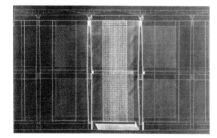

Fig. 2.4
High School; sunscreens on classroom facades, detail.

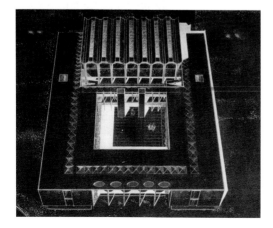

Fig. 2.3
High School;
aerial perspective.

GRADUATE SCHOOL AND APPRENTICESHIP

along a highway in Connecticut is unlike any of Ernest's other Yale projects but is similar to his University of Virginia thesis project, which may place it near the beginning of his time at Yale. The site is accessed by off-ramps from the highway, and the circular, earth-bermed restaurant is set towards the edge of the much larger circular site at the farthest point from the highway (fig. 2.5). The site consists of a series of organically curved, earth-bermed parking areas wrapping the perimeter and folding inwards to form four triangular terraces. Ernest renders the hand-colored site plan with brown and tan paved parking areas, green landscape berms, and white pedestrian pathways (fig. 2.6). The circular landscaped site is in turn completely covered by a high roof made of a grid of translucent glass canopies, hexagonal in plan and diamond-shaped in section, which are each supported at their centers on steel posts set in a triangular grid (fig. 2.7). During the day the translucent roof canopy was intended to cast a cloud-like shadow, filled with dim light, over the site, while at night the artificial lighting within the diamond-shaped, hexagonal glass volumes would illuminate the site in a moonlight-like glow.

The subterranean restaurant has two levels that are organized around the double-height "skylight dome" at the center of the plan (fig. 2.8). On the lower entry level, the down-sloping entrance ramp arrives at an elongated bar that wraps both sides and swells out at the center, and the restrooms are housed in cylindrical volumes framing the entry portal. On the upper level, which is accessed by a double ramp wrapping around both sides of the skylight dome at the center, dining tables are arranged on the circular floor. The only opening in the translucent hexagonal canopy that covers the entire site is over the skylight dome at the center of the restaurant. The subterranean structure is made of concrete walls and piers that curve organically in both plan and section, branching and thickening in response to structural requirements, including the weight and pressure of earth and groundwater on the walls and ceiling.

Ernest's design for the restaurant and its site is a remarkably resolved example of what would be later called "earth architecture," with its attributes of reduced energy consumption, integration with natural topography and vegetation, and emphasis on stereotomic spaces carved into the landscape (rather than object-buildings placed on top of the landscape), which can be related to examples of the ancient mound-building tradition to be found throughout the Americas.[20] While the restaurant was his only project with organic curving surfaces, Ernest would return to the idea of hexagonal-plan and diamond-section roof canopies in several of his later Florida projects. Rather than being related to any of Rudolph or Kahn's contemporary projects, Ernest's design is quite close in spirit to Eero Saarinen's TWA Terminal in Queens, New York, which was then in construction. It is worth noting that at this same time Saarinen was beginning work on the Stiles and Morse residential colleges (dormitories) at Yale.

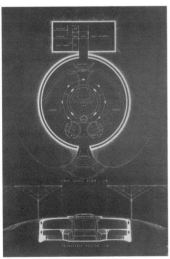

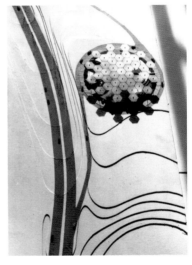

Fig. 2.7
Restaurant Yale project, ca. 1958; exterior
perspective of earth mounds and roof canopy.
Fig. 2.8
Restaurant; first-floor plan (above),
transverse section (below).
Fig. 2.5
Restaurant; site model with motorway.
Fig. 2.6
Restaurant; site and landscape plan.

GRADUATE SCHOOL AND APPRENTICESHIP

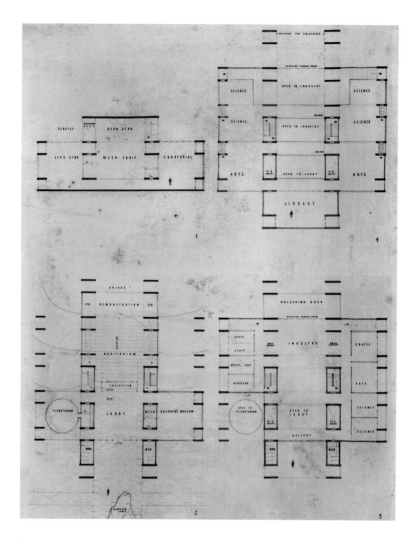

Fig. 2.9 Museum of Science and Industry, Bridgeport, Connecticut,
Yale project, ca. 1958; floorplans.

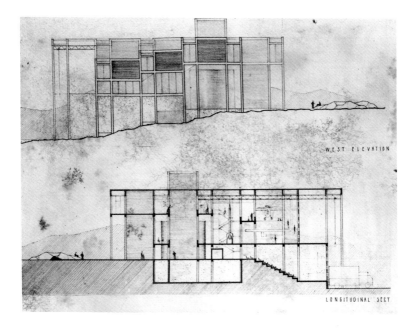

Fig. 2.10 Museum; west elevation (above) and longitudinal section (below).

In designing a museum of science and industry, on a steep north-sloping site on Park Avenue overlooking Veterans Memorial Park in Bridgeport, Connecticut, Ernest and his fellow Master Class students were given the program and site for an actual project, built some years later. Ernest's design for the multistory museum is organized into a cruciform plan that is ordered by a tartan grid of alternating narrow bays and wide bays in both directions, with the primary spaces running down the center from south to north and secondary spaces flanking them to the east and west. The narrower ten-foot bays house solid concrete structural pier walls, service, and circulation spaces, while the wider bays, varying from thirty to forty feet, house the primary museum galleries of science, arts, and industry, as well as the cylindrical planetarium, entry, and library (figs. 2.9 and 2.10).

The entry of the museum is a monumental gateway or portico formed by two pairs of concrete pier walls supporting the library at the top level. The ceiling of the main central space of the museum, which is the same height as the entry, extends the length of the museum, while the floor steps down the slope to form an auditorium and a loading area at the bottom of the hill. The loading area, fitted with airplane hangar doors, is large enough to accept a full-scale aircraft. The smaller elevated galleries along the two sides step down with the slope and are linked by bridges crossing the central space, forming a complex interlocking section shown in Ernest's perspectives of interior views looking down the central space and stepping section from south to north (fig. 2.11) and across one of the bridges that span from side to side at the upper levels.

The building is structured by a series of pairs of ten-by-one-foot concrete pier walls framing the major central spaces, and pairs of eight-by-one-foot concrete pier walls at the periphery, with the museum rooms spanning between. The model indicates Ernest's intention to articulate the structural frame of the paired pier walls on the exterior, clearly differentiating between the load-bearing piers (in light gray) and the load-borne volumes spanning between (in darker gray). The photographs Ernest made of the stages of building the model intentionally parallel the process of construction from the ground up, emphasizing the importance of the concrete pier walls, which were to be built first (fig. 2.12).

The similarities between the structural order of the twenty-five-year-old Ernest's design and the fifty-seven-year-old Kahn's only-then-emerging way of structuring space are indeed striking, as Kahn himself first engaged the tartan grid in his plans for the main building of the Trenton Jewish Community Center of 1956–58, based on the earlier Bath House with its concrete block pier walls framing the primary spaces. In his seminal 1962 book on Kahn, Ernest's professor Vincent Scully would point out that the tartan grid and cruciform (or "cross-axial") plan of the Bath House, which he correctly identified as Kahn's breakthrough project — where he argued Kahn discovered a way of beginning anew—were both shared with Wright's own early Prairie-Period projects.[21] It was around this time that Kahn first called this type of tartan patterning of the floor plan, based in his case on studying the plans of Palladio and Wright, the "servant" and "served" spaces, an insight he passed on to his students.

Ernest's design for the redevelopment of a downtown New Haven city block, bounded by High, Crown, Chapel, and College Streets and across Chapel Street from the Yale campus, proposed new buildings with housing along High Street and parking garages (which use car elevators rather than ramps) along Crown Street, all of which were to have commercial space on the ground floor. The project retained an existing commercial building on High Street and the College Street Music Hall, dating to 1926, located at the center of the block, as well as the existing buildings on Chapel Street. A plan diagram and a model composed of stacked wooden blocks document the project's potential extension to include all of High and Chapel Streets (fig. 2.13), but the final drawings all relate to the more limited intervention incorporating the existing buildings.

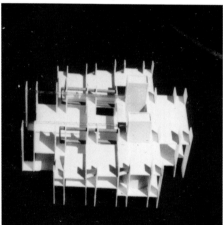

Fig. 2.11
Museum; interior perspective.
Fig. 2.12
Museum; study model showing
structural piers.

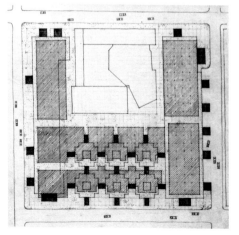

Fig. 2.13
Urban block redevelopment, New
Haven, Connecticut, Yale project,
ca. 1959; site plan of fully extended
project.

GRADUATE SCHOOL AND APPRENTICESHIP

This is one of only two projects in Ernest's archives that include his design process sketches, the other being his own house in Florida (1960–61). The sketches document Ernest's exhaustive exploration of possible ways of organizing the housing, including variations in the stacking of the apartments, with apartments spanning between adjacent pairs of stair towers at alternate floors (forming overlapping "neighborhoods" aboveground and open courts at the center of each cluster) and the stair towers clustering around the apartments (as in the final design, with courts linking the outer corners of four clusters) (figs. 2.14, 2.15, and 2.16). The sketches also include variations in the positioning of the stair towers, with the towers at the corners (documented with a small, eye-level perspective, as seen from the street) and at the center of the apartment clusters (as in the final design). The designs with the stair towers at the corners of the apartment clusters produce a more uniform and continuous street front, whereas the designs with the stair towers at the center of the apartment clusters produce a more varied street front, with the buildings shifting in and out of alignment with the sidewalk edge. All Ernest's design variations maintained a high degree of porosity in plan and section, providing all apartments generous sunlight and cross-ventilating breezes, as well as a substantial exterior terrace.

In the plans, sections, and elevations presenting the final design, the housing is organized as cruciform-plan, four-floor clusters, in which the upper three floors contain residential apartments and the higher ground floor contains commercial space, with four brick, masonry-walled stair towers connecting the apartment clusters at the center of each edge (fig. 2.17). The three floors of housing, each containing three apartments (one three-bedroom and two studios), are rectangular in plan, with their short sides extending to connect to two of the stair towers, which provide access, the stair sets alternating at each floor. In each apartment, the service core of kitchens and baths are clustered in a square volume set against the solid central wall, while the outer corners of their L-shaped plans are cantilevered.[22] The three floors of apartments rotate 90 degrees as they rise, allowing the roofs of the apartments below to be used as terraces.[23] The outer corners of the floors and ceilings of the apartments are cantilevered from the beam pairs running between the stair towers, and Ernest emphasizes the lack of columns in the open corners by butt-glazing them—two full-height pieces of glass meeting at the corner with no mullion.

In his High Street elevation, Ernest stepped his buildings down from the highest on the corner at Crown Street to the lowest adjacent to the existing commercial block, which itself steps down to the corner of Chapel Street (fig. 2.18). Concrete corner columns and floor slabs frame the towers' brick infill walls, which help integrate the project with the vertical brick masses of the existing commercial building. The combination

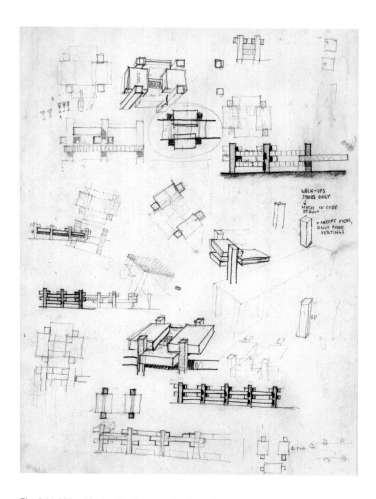

Fig. 2.14 Urban block redevelopment; sketches of apartment towers.

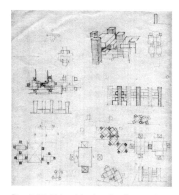

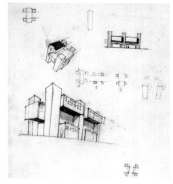

Fig. 2.15 Urban block redevelopment; sketches of apartment towers.

Fig. 2.16 Sketches and perspective

GRADUATE SCHOOL AND APPRENTICESHIP

44

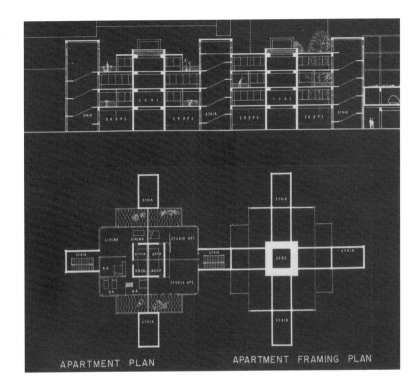

Fig. 2.17 Urban block redevelopment; apartment towers section (above) and floorplan and structural diagram (below).

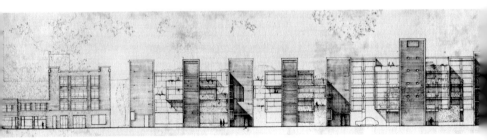

Fig. 2.18 Urban block redevelopment; Chapel Street elevation.

A MOMENT IN THE SUN

of the thin, widely spaced, projecting, brick-walled stair towers, the spaces opened in section at the apartment terraces, and the forecourts formed in plan by the stepping back of each apartment cluster, results in the majority of the street front opening to the spaces in the interior of the block—a porous counterpoint to the traditional street wall. From the overall strategy of independent towers with cantilevered corners serviced by four solid-walled stair towers connecting them at the center of each edge to details such as the butt-glazed corners and stepped concrete cantilever beams, the design is strongly influenced by Kahn's University of Pennsylvania Richards Medical Laboratory towers, then in construction—a project which Rudolph encouraged his students to visit.

A direct connection to Kahn is found in the pages of Ernest's sketchbook for this project, where on the reverse side of a page of pencil sketches there are notes in ink documenting Kahn's comments during a lecture (either at Yale or University of Pennsylvania), in which Kahn spoke about his "Plan for Midtown Philadelphia" of 1952–53 and his "Civic Center for Philadelphia" of 1957. Ernest carefully notes Kahn's proposal of "Go" streets for through traffic, with no parking or busses; "Stop" streets for busses, service, and parking; and large parking garages as "Docks" (Kahn called them "wound-up streets") along the periphery to accept the expressway traffic and house large commercial shops and how all of these allow the remaining central city streets to become exclusively pedestrian ways. Next to these notes in Ernest's sketchbook is a plan drawing labeled "row houses" showing Kahn's 1953 public housing project for the Philadelphia City Planning Commission, in which the basic unit is a cluster of five row house blocks, each with its own parking area, arranged around a hexagonal garden at the center that opens at its end to the access road. Triangular gardens at the back of each of the five row house blocks links them to two adjacent hexagonal clusters of five row house blocks, forming a weaving pattern that takes advantage of the interlocking geometry of triangles and hexagons—one of Ernest's favorite spatial themes.[24]

Ernest's thesis project, a new City Hall for New Haven, was sited on Church Street across from and fronting onto the New Haven Green with its three historic churches, to the northwest (fig. 2.19). Ernest's design for the 90,000-square-foot program involved forming a large rectangular entry and assembly plaza that opened off Church Street, and where beneath the porous grate-like paving, two floors of secured parking were located. The new public plaza, sized to accommodate major public events and political gatherings, was framed on both sides by existing buildings and at the rear by an elongated five-story slab, running perpendicular to Church Street and set back to the mid-point of the urban block, which contained the office spaces, the largest part of the City Hall program (fig. 2.20). The public hearing rooms and courtrooms were gathered in a cantilevered tower, equal in height to the four floors of offices and structured by four central service towers, that was set as a freestanding volume in the open space behind the elongated office slab, fronting onto Orange Street to the southeast (figs. 2.21 and 2.22). Rising to the full height of the office block and framed by two pairs of deep, massive pier walls, the entry hall for both the office slab and the public assembly room tower was located at the intersection of the elongated office slab volume and the central axis of the Green, with which the public assembly room tower was aligned (figs. 2.23, 2.24 and 2.25). A new pedestrian underpass led from the Green across the street, through a sunken courtyard in the plaza, and then beneath the entry hall to terminate in the public assembly room building at the rear.

The eleven bays of the elongated City Hall office slab are structured with large concrete piers, set in front of the porous facade, which rise the full height of the building from beneath the plaza floor to the deep overhanging roof. As shown in Ernest's carefully rendered section and elevation, the five concrete floors of the office block are recessed and the concrete beams supporting them are secured to the rear face of the concrete piers at the front and back of the building, with a series of smaller interior columns supporting the floors running down the center of the building (fig.2.26). Beneath the roof, the ceremonial and honorific rooms of the taller, more open top floor are spaced away to provide gardens between, with the mayor's office being cantilevered out of the central, sixth bay, while the council chamber is located in a glass cylinder in the third bay, and the full height entry hall is recessed into the ninth bay.

The porous floor of the plaza is mirrored in the porous front facade of the lower four floors of the elongated office slab, and the woven panel fabric of the facade divides each floor level into three offset window slots. This is emphasized in the night photographs of the model, with the light coming out from within the glowing building. Due to the way Ernest recesses the facade behind the piers, thereby hiding the structural connections of the floors, the whole woven vertical surface hovers above the plaza, diminishing its apparent mass while allowing natural light into the subterranean spaces of the police department beneath. In contrast, the enormous void of the entry hall, framed by the massive pier walls and rising to the full height of the building, appears to have been carved from the body of the building (fig. 2.27). The soaring entry hall allows those entering to see, framed by the massive pier walls and oversailing roof, the tower housing the public meeting and court rooms, contrasting the post and beam structure of the office building to the cantilevered structure of the public assembly room tower beyond. Ernest's design employs the monumental scale of the building, largely comprised of repetitive small-scale office space, to frame the large plaza it forms, which is a true space of public appearance for the citizens of New Haven.

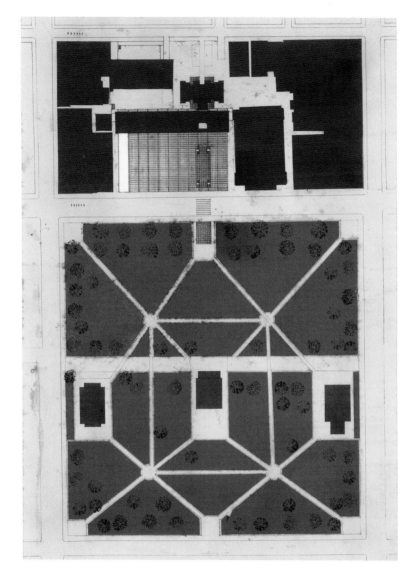

Fig. 2.19 Thesis project for City Hall, New Haven, Connecticut, Yale project, 1959; site plan with New Haven Green (below) and proposed City Hall (above).

GRADUATE SCHOOL AND APPRENTICESHIP

Fig. 2.20 City Hall; perspective of City Hall as seen from New Haven Green, note pedestrian underpass beneath Church Street, in foreground.

Fig. 2.21 City Hall; model, aerial view from west.

Fig. 2.22 City Hall; model, view of plaza and entry hall.

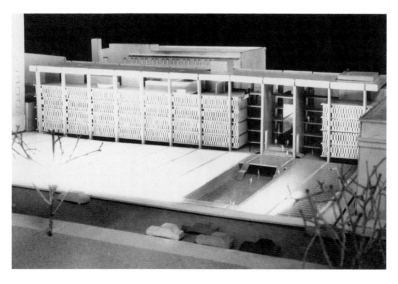

GRADUATE SCHOOL AND APPRENTICESHIP

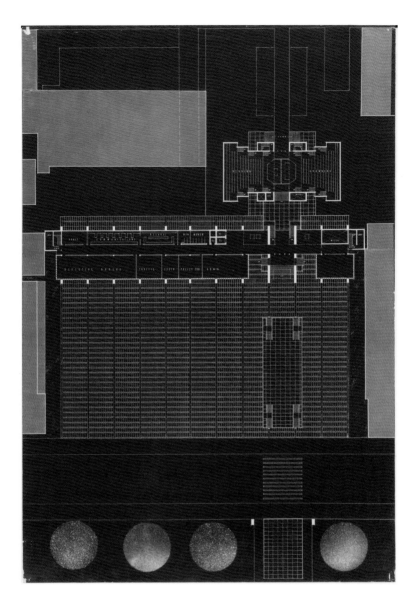

Fig. 2.23 City Hall; ground-floor plan with plaza.

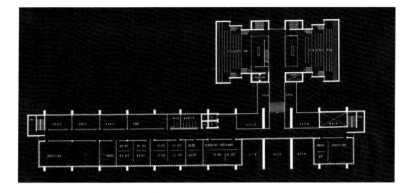

Fig. 2.45 City Hall; courts-level plan.

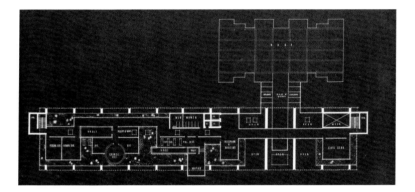

Fig. 2.25 City Hall; top-floor plan, with city council and mayor's office.

Ernest's full-height piers structuring the multistory office slab, which imparts a monumentality beyond the building's actual scale, may be related to the similar elements in Rudolph's Deering House of 1958 and Sarasota High School, then in construction. The massive, deep pier walls that frame the full-height entry hall and rise to support the oversailing roof of Ernest's City Hall may be related to the (admittedly far more sculptural) entry canopy and piers of Le Corbusier's Assembly Building at Chandigarh, India, the construction of which was well underway. Ernest's treatment of the open, upper floor of the office slab may also be related to Le Corbusier's similar distribution of free-form volumes at the rooftop in projects such as the early Salvation Army in Paris—with the important caveat that Ernest's top floor is an interior rather than an exterior space, covered by the enormous roof canopy and opening to the city.

There is an unidentified project in Ernest's portfolio of the work that is not included on any of the lists of his works made during his lifetime,

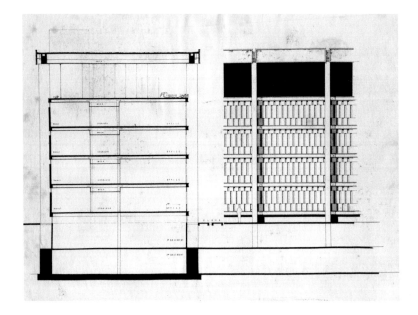

Fig. 2.26 City Hall; section (left) and elevation detail (right) facing plaza.

Fig. 2.27 City Hall; model, view of plaza, entry hall, and office slab facade.

and which is most likely an independent competition design undertaken while he was in Rudolph's Master Class program at Yale.[25] The project, documented in three floor plans and photographs of one model, is for a large institutional program on a waterfront site that steps in section (fig. 2.28). Exactly what program the building is designed to house is not clear, though its organization is perhaps closest to a conference center. The building has two parts, a larger triangular plan building that extends out into the water, with the land shaped to its angled form, which is three stories in height—water level, ground level, and upper level, and a smaller cruciform-in-square plan building that is set on the land, which is two stories in height above the ground, with one basement set at the water level (figs. 2.29, 2.30, and 2.31). The only link between the two buildings is the canopy-covered portico at the ground or middle level that spans between them and shelters the entries to both buildings which open off of it (similar to Wright's Unity Temple). Assuming the site is in the northern hemisphere, the shadows in the model photographs suggest that the larger triangular building is located to the north and the smaller rectangular building is located to the south.

The larger triangular building is entered from beneath the portico canopy by moving on axis from south to north through banks of glass doors set between wall-like blocks of smaller rooms and directly into the middle level. Pier walls set on the 60-degree grid of the building rise from the water level below to the ceiling two levels above, and openings cut in the ground-floor slab allow light to penetrate to the lower water level. To either side, rectangular rooms, alternating larger and smaller, line the two angled outer walls overlooking the water, with each of the larger rooms closed to the central room by what appears to be closet walls and with entries on either side from in front of the smaller rooms. The same alternating rooms also line the two angled sides of the mezzanine at the upper level above. The center of the main room houses two triangular clusters of three rooms, each room aligning with one of the three pier walls that rise to the roof. The lower level, which appears to open without glazing to the waterfront through the piers supporting the rooms along the periphery of the ground and upper floors, has pairs of U-shaped walls framing a seemingly unprogrammed space beneath the triangular room clusters above. The three levels are connected by four triangular stairs housed in cylindrical volumes, though it is not clear whether these cylinders are solid-walled or circular holes cut in the ground and upper-level floor slabs. At the upper level, these cylindrical stairs are centered in triangular floor sections that link to the linear mezzanines ringing the double-height central room.

Directly across from the entry, a single pier wall marks the center of the main room and aligns with the wide bridge, spanning across the space opening to the lower level, which leads to the auditorium entrance.

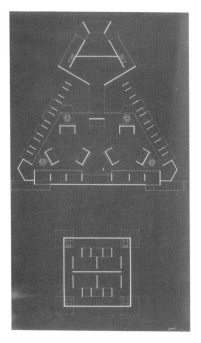

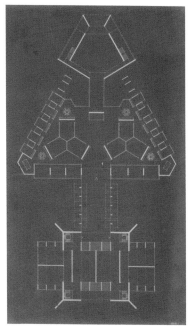

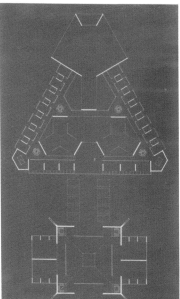

Fig. 2.29
Unidentified project;
lower, water-level floorplan.
Fig. 2.30
Unidentified project;
main, ground-level floorplan.
Fig. 2.31
Unidentified project;
upper-level floorplan.

Fig. 2.28 Unidentified project, ca. 1959; model with roof removed.

GRADUATE SCHOOL AND APPRENTICESHIP

The large triangular auditorium is placed at the pier-like end of the triangular building, its floor sloping down towards the water to the north—though there are no seats shown in the plans. The height of the three pairs of massive pier walls framing the back, sides, and front of this auditorium, which rise to two and three times the height of any other walls in the model, indicate that this tallest room, set out into the water and rising from its floor at water level to its roofs well above the height of the rest of the building, was the focus of the institution.

Entry to the smaller, cruciform-in-square plan building is also from the ground-level portico, but after passing between the outer walls, the central axis is blocked by solid volumes, so the pair of entries open to either side. Four square stairs, set in the outer corners of the main square, provide access to the upper and lower basement levels. On the ground floor, the central square space is divided by partitions that do not touch the outer walls, including one running down the center, suggesting that this building houses galleries or display spaces. At the ground and upper levels, gallery-like rooms, structured by pier walls, are set in wings opening to the east and west, parallel to the waterfront volume. On the upper level, the central square space houses a single large, undivided gallery, covered by a pyramid roof with an oculus at the center (similar to Kahn's contemporary Trenton Jewish Community Center), and the four diagonal roof beams are supported on angled abutments that extend from the outer corners of the building. On the lower basement level, the square space is again given partitions, and two sets of three small rooms appear to receive light through the glass block–filled openings in the floor above.

The project is the closest to Kahn's work of any of Ernest's designs, as evidenced by Ernest's use of four triangular stairs housed in cylindrical volumes—exact matches for the main stair in Kahn's Yale Art Gallery, where Ernest was sitting in studio during his time in the Yale Master Class. This astonishingly resolved design also closely parallels a number of Kahn's contemporary projects, including the Adath Jeshurun Synagogue project and the Goldenberg House, as well as presaging several of Kahn's later works, including the President's Estate in Islamabad, Pakistan. In addition, both the program and the waterfront site of Ernest's design have intriguing parallels with the "Interama" project for an international exhibition and cultural center in Miami, but Kahn started working on that project in 1963, after Ernest's death. The design's remarkable parallels with Kahn's later, mature works, as well as Ernest's superb resolution of its Kahn-like geometries, make this unidentified project the clearest indication we have that by spring 1959, at the age of twenty-six, Ernest was designing buildings that compare favorably with the works of the very best architects then practicing.

After receiving his master of architecture degree from Yale University, Ernest worked from June 1959 to June 1960 in Memphis, Tennessee, for Mann and Harrover, Architects.[26] The firm was headed by William Mann and Roy Perkins Harrover, the latter a 1953 graduate of Yale, where he had been in Kahn's design studio, had taken Vincent Scully's history courses, and had Philip Johnson and Buckminster Fuller as visiting critics. Ernest worked on at least three building designs during his year with the firm, one of which won the competition held for its commission, and was subsequently realized, and the other two of which later won *Progressive Architecture* Awards, one of the most prestigious awards for architectural designs in the United States.

The first of the three buildings on which Ernest worked was the Memphis Art Academy, which Mann and Harrover won in a 1959 competition, their design having been selected by the jury that included Paul Rudolph (Ernest's professor at Yale) and Philip Johnson (Harrover's professor at Yale). The building, which is still in use today as the Memphis College of Art, comprises two brick-walled volumes opening to a central court between them, the whole surrounded by projected vertical concrete sunscreens and covered by a folded plate concrete roof canopy very similar to that of the High School project Ernest designed in Rudolph's Master Class. However, this project was not documented by Ernest in his portfolio, which most likely indicates that he did not consider himself the primary designer, unlike the other two projects.

The design for the Memphis Municipal Airport Terminal Complex is credited to Ernest and his Yale classmate, Donald Winkelmann (who in 1961 went on to become the design partner of Naramore, Bain, Brady, and Johanson (NBBJ) in Seattle), as project co-designers, as cited in the *Progressive Architecture* awards issue. A note in Ernest's portfolio states that Winkelmann had primary responsibility for the central terminal, while the multilevel extended concourses were Ernest's design. The program called for a compact but expandable terminal for the city of 500,000, located on a narrow band of land between two existing roadways. The "head and tail" scheme of the airport locates the terminal to the north, fronting onto a parking plaza, around the perimeter of which a ramped roadway brings automobiles to the main middle level of the terminal for both arrival and departure (figs. 2.32 and 2.33). The terminal building is organized on three levels, with airport service on the ground level, passenger circulation and check-in on the main middle level, and a perimeter mezzanine on the top level. The main lower volume of the terminal, which runs east to west along the access roadway, is constructed with concrete structural columns and frame with brick infill walls. The public spaces of the terminal are covered by an elevated roof canopy of

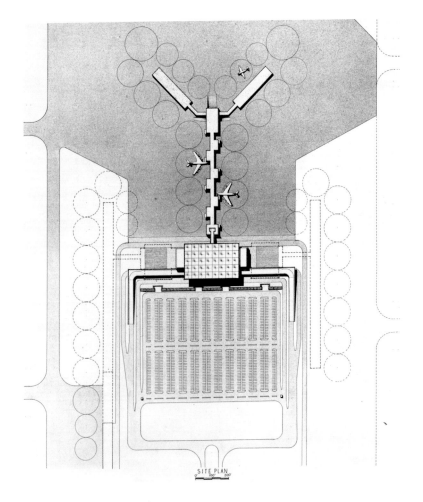

Fig. 2.32 Memphis Airport, Memphis, Tennessee, MH Architects, 1959–60; site plan.

A MOMENT IN THE SUN

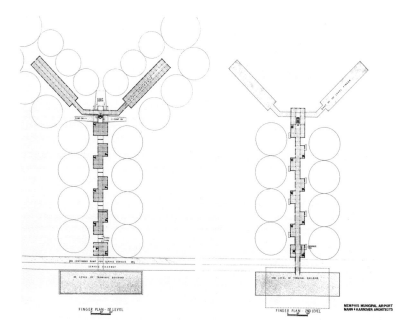

Fig. 2.35 Memphis Airport; concourse first, ground-floor plan (left) and second, upper-floor plan (right).

Fig. 2.33 Memphis Airport; aerial perspective of new terminal.
Fig. 2.34 Memphis Airport; perspective of terminal (left) and concourse (right).

hyperbolic-paraboloid thin-shell concrete vaults, supported by exposed cast concrete columns, and entirely glazed around the perimeter, which spans across the lower volume from south to north and forms the ceiling for the double-height passenger level and the mezzanine (fig. 2.34).

A two-level linear concourse, called the "Finger Plan" on the drawings, extends from the main terminal to the south, with the ground, service, and operations level regularly opened by passages to allow vehicle access to both sides (fig. 2.35). The upper passenger boarding level is organized into boarding lounges, equipped with bridges for boarding and deplaning larger planes, which alternate to the east and west along the concourse's length. The upper level of the linear concourse terminates in a double-height stair hall through which passengers descend to the Y-shaped ground-level concourse for the boarding and deplaning of smaller planes on the tarmac. The concourse is constructed with concrete structural columns and frame and brick infill walls, and the concourse's walls fold seamlessly into the lower walls of the main volume of the terminal. A rooftop walkway extends from the perimeter of the mezzanine level of the terminal, beneath the thin shell roof canopy, to the observation

GRADUATE SCHOOL AND APPRENTICESHIP

terrace on top of the concourse roof. Ernest's portion of the design was one of the first uses of linear concourses and two-level access, with passengers above ground service, for a smaller, multipurpose airport. The airport is still in use and has been expanded by adding to both the concourse arms and to either side of the main terminal. While the design responsibility was divided between Winkelmann and Ernest as noted above, the perspective drawings submitted for the *Progressive Architecture* Award appear to have been drawn in Ernest's distinctive manner.

The design of the Memphis Speech and Hearing Center for the State of Tennessee is credited to Ernest in the *Progressive Architecture* awards issue. The large and demanding program, as well as surface parking, was required to be accommodated on a very tight site within an existing regional medical complex, and it had to be realized within a very limited budget. The program involves laboratories for acoustic testing for hearing, numerous rooms for speech therapy, rooms for training of speech and hearing technicians enrolled in the adjacent medical school, classrooms for nursery and elementary school speech and hearing patients, conference room, offices, social and vocational counseling, administrative and staff spaces, research workshops, entry hall and waiting room, and auditorium—all of which needed to be acoustically isolated to eliminate sound transmission between rooms. Ernest's design places the majority of the program spaces within a two-story, golden section-shaped plan, the rooms ordered by the introduction of a central cruciform intersecting north-south and east-west at the entry hall, with the acoustic testing spaces in a separate building, structurally and acoustically isolated from the main building, set to the south (figs. 2.36 and 2.37). The three classrooms at the basement level open to the sunken court to the south. To minimize sound transmission, brick cavity bearing walls, with brick outside and inside, support concrete beams and floor slabs, with wide and narrow windows cut into the walls between the concrete floor beams.

Despite the complex, densely packed program and its requirement for many solid, acoustically insulating walls, the building is centered on large, generously illuminated central rooms on two levels, with the expansive entry hall below and glass-walled auditorium above, both of which are opened internally to both the east and west, and externally to the north and south (fig. 2.38). Brick piers running north-south frame the entry hall on the ground floor and the auditorium on the upper floor, with wide hallways running east-west set on the other side of the piers. The ceilings of the hallways are lowered to accommodate the mechanical ducts, which also emphasizes the primacy of the larger rooms on either side of the hallways. To the north of the entry hall a large sunken court separates the central block of rooms from the one-story acoustic testing building to the south, and the main staircases are set to either side of the

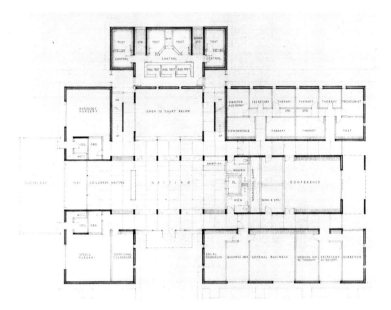

Fig. 2.36 Speech and Hearing Center, Memphis, Tennessee, MH Architects, 1959–60; first-floor plan.

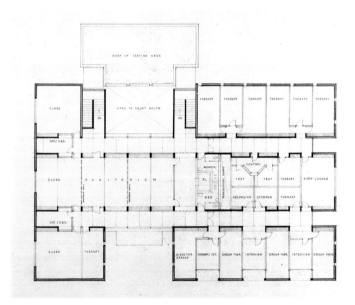

Fig. 2.37 Speech and Hearing Center; second-floor plan.

GRADUATE SCHOOL AND APPRENTICESHIP

court. Public entry takes place along the building's central axis, passing through the large, recessed court to the north, beneath the canopy and through the glazed doors. Staff entry takes place on either side from the south, through the pair of entry vestibules at the rear of the staircases that give access to both the main building and the acoustic testing building (figs. 2.39 and 2.40).

Daylight and exterior views are introduced into the center of the building in a number of ways: first, by the deeply recessed courts on both sides of the entry hall and auditorium, the entry court on the north side, and the large, sunken court on the south side, which also brings generous daylight to the three classrooms on the lower basement level; second, through the children's waiting area from the children's play court recessed into the east end of the building, and introduced into the staff area and conference room through the staff terrace recessed into the west end of the building; third, by the fully glazed western ends of the hallways at the ground and upper floor and the use of wide and narrow full-height window openings throughout to provide the necessary differing degrees of privacy to the spaces within; and fourth, by the deep clerestory windows running continuously beneath the roof on the north and south sides of the auditorium at the top of the building. The floor plans and sections, ordered by a two-directional tartan grid of alternating narrow bands of circulation and service spaces and wide bands of primary spaces, is remarkably resolved, resulting in open, naturally illuminated, easily navigable interior spaces that allow both visual and physical movement for the patients, many of whom have impaired hearing and thus rely on their vision.

Six months after Ernest left Mann and Harrover to move back to Florida, the January 1961 issue of *Progressive Architecture* announced the 8th Annual *Progressive Architecture* Awards, selected by a jury of Philip Johnson, Walter Netsch (Skidmore, Owings, and Merrill, Chicago), Chloethiel Woodard Smith (Satterlee and Smith, DC), O'Neil Ford (San Antonio), and Charles Colbert (Colbert, Lowry, Hess, Boudreau, New Orleans, and dean of Architecture at Columbia University). Buildings designed by Ernest won an unprecedented three of the eighteen awards given among the 507 entries received: the Memphis Municipal Airport, the Memphis Speech and Hearing Center, and the Robert Ernest House, Atlantic Beach, Florida. Two of the three buildings were designed before Ernest reached his twenty-seventh birthday, and it is hard to imagine more convincing evidence of Ernest's remarkable talent and great potential as an architect.

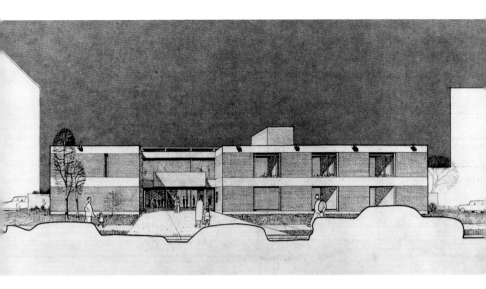

Fig. 2.39 Speech and Hearing Center; perspective of front elevation.

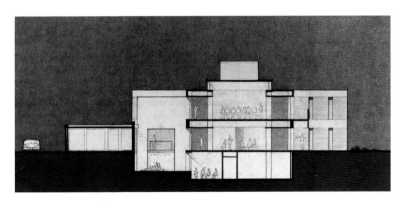

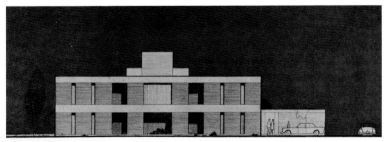

Fig. 2.38 Speech and Hearing Center; section.
Fig. 2.40 Speech and Hearing Center; side elevation.

Fig. 3a.14 Ernest House; interior view looking from living/dining room down into double-height studio.

Robert Ernest, Architect, Jacksonville, Florida

In June 1960 Ernest moved back to Jacksonville, Florida, to establish his own practice, having been contracted by Paul Rudolph to supervise the construction of what would prove to be Rudolph's last house realized in Florida, the Milam House in nearby Ponte Vedra (1959–61). The fact that Rudolph would entrust this important task to Ernest clearly indicates that even though Ernest had only graduated from Yale one year before, Rudolph already had the highest respect for Ernest's qualities as a designer, his knowledge of construction, and his ability to realize Rudolph's designs appropriately and precisely—this last dating back to Ernest's two summers working in Rudolph's Cambridge and Sarasota offices, as well as his year at Yale. When Rudolph's Milam House won a Record Houses Award, announced in the May 1963 issue of *Architectural Record*, Ernest was posthumously credited as "supervising architect."

In his design for the Milam House on its oceanfront site, Rudolph engaged and expanded upon Le Corbusier's concept of the applied sunscreen or *brise-soleil* to generate a remarkably resolved spatial and formal design. The largely solid, planar, western entry facade and the largely open, monumental, plastically powerful, eastern ocean-facing facade form outer layers of interlocking spatial units that are drawn back through the interior to structure the plan and shape the section (figs. 3.1, 3.2, and 3.3). The eastern facade of the house also marks a change in Rudolph's characteristic formal expression, moving from single, larger rectangular volumes divided into regular bays to a more sculpturally dynamic clustering of differently scaled rectangular volumes. That the walls of this exceptional house and its sunscreens were built almost entirely of locally manufactured, tan-colored concrete blocks, with cast-in-place concrete edge beams and floor slabs, would serve as an inspiration for Ernest's own works, as well as for later developments in Florida architecture.

In parallel to this work for Rudolph, Ernest also set up his own independent architectural practice in Jacksonville in the summer of 1960. Ernest's first office was located in a small boat dock house on the west shore of the St. John's River in the yard of his parents' house in Jacksonville at 1880 Powell Place, Riverside, southwest of downtown. In the next twenty-three months, until his death in May 1962, Ernest would see two of his designs constructed, the Robert Ernest and Eli Becker Houses and a third design days away from starting construction, the Jacksonville Youth Center. He would also design at least ten commissioned projects, several of which were set to begin construction at the time of his death, but all of which remained unbuilt after his passing.

Fig. 3.3 Milam House; interior of living room.
Fig. 3.2 Milam House; exterior view from beach.

Fig. 3.1 Milam House, Ponte Vedra, Florida, 1961, Paul Rudolph; perspective.

ARCHITECTURAL PRACTICE

Robert and Lynwood Ernest House and Studio, Atlantic Beach, Florida, 1960-61

The first of the three designs Ernest realized was for his own residence and architectural studio in Atlantic Beach, an oceanfront community to the east of Jacksonville. Built on a narrow, 50-by-138-foot lot, oriented east-west and accessed from Beach Avenue to the east and Ocean Boulevard to the west, the house is without beach frontage, separated from the ocean by a row of houses to the east. To provide the main rooms with a view of the ocean over the beachfront houses to the east, Ernest proposed a three-story house, with the studio on the first level, the living room and screened porch at the second level, and the bedrooms on the third level. Ernest positioned the house at the eastern end of the lot, closer to the ocean and Beach Avenue, with a garden, guest parking and entry on the western side, off Ocean Boulevard (figs. 3a.1, 3a.2, 3a.3, and 3a.4). (The first four illustrations are the drawings that Ernest submitted in fall 1960 to the 8th Annual *Progressive Architecture* Awards for designs not yet built).

Before arriving at the final design, Ernest explored a series of alternatives in both plan and section. In plan, Ernest sketched a series of three- and five-equal-bay schemes, formed by parallel walls running east-west, with interior, enclosed spaces and exterior, open-air spaces shifting east and west to form a T-shaped cluster of interior spaces on the ocean side, with a central space with carports to either side on the west side. But soon Ernest likely realized that these wider groupings of spaces would not fit on the narrow, 50-foot-wide site, given the required 7.5-foot setbacks from the north and south property lines, which, in addition, are slightly angled with respect to Ocean Boulevard and Beach Avenue, thus leaving less than a 35-foot-wide buildable area.

Ernest developed two versions of a three-bay plan, both of which have a wide bay in the center, opening to the east and west, and two narrow bays to the north and south. In the first version, the parallel walls defining all three bays extend the full length of the plan, in the form of a rectangle, with the wide primary rooms placed in a staggered section at the center, and the narrow bays on either side used for stairs, services, and storage. In the second version, the narrower outer bays are shortened and occupy the middle of the plan, which now takes the form of a cruciform, and the wider central bay is separated from the outer bays by a thickened, in-folded wall containing the primary structure, stairs, services, and storage (fig. 3a.2).

The final plan was developed from the second cruciform-shaped scheme, but it is the east-west section through the center of the house that sets it apart from other contemporary buildings (fig. 3a.3). In parallel to the plan developments, Ernest explored a series of section compositions for the twenty-four-foot-tall and thirty-eight-foot-long central

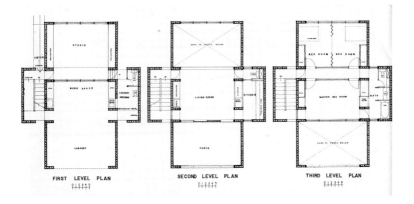

Fig. 3a.2 Ernest House; preliminary floorplans.

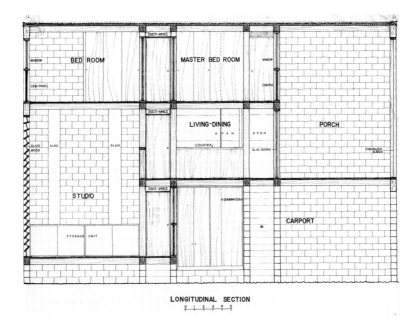

Fig. 3a.3 Ernest House; preliminary section.

Next page:

Fig. 3a.1 Ernest House, Atlantic Beach, Florida, 1960–61; perspective of eastern, ocean side.

ARCHITECTURAL PRACTICE

ERNEST

volume (a golden section, which was clearly an intentional decision on Ernest's part), with interlocking single- and double-height spaces. All the sections for the house that are recorded in Ernest's sketches employ a variation on the section from Le Corbusier's first unrealized design for the so-called "Carthage Villa" (1928), which was also for an oceanfront site. This now-canonical section consists of a series of double-height spaces, each occupying one-third of the floor, which are offset by one level and alternated from one side of the house to the other, thereby spatially connecting the rooms on all levels of the house. In Le Corbusier's five-story design, the upper four floors are interlocked by three overlapping double-height spaces to form a stacked Z-shaped space in section, which rises from the second to the fifth floor, with a single- and double-height, covered, open-air terrace at the top. The complex staggered pattern of single- and double-height windows at the narrow, almost entirely glazed end facades of the house open to the ocean view.[27]

Despite being both height limited, by code, and budget limited, by necessity, to three floors maximum, Ernest's first sections are remarkably close to the upper four floors of Le Corbusier's first Carthage Villa design. In these initial section sketches, the double-height studio, the lowest room in the section, is lifted several feet off the ground, and the open-air carport is placed beneath the double-height living room. The single-height children's bedrooms are placed over the studio, with the single-height parent's bedroom, a half-level up, placed over the living room, and a low-walled roof terrace, another half-level up, is placed above the children's bedroom. There are at least twelve design variations on this initial section, all of which explore the idea of placing 4.5 levels of rooms into what is effectively only three floors, each eight feet in height, through the use of the split- or half-level organization (fig. 3a.5). Several of the sections also have shallow terraces with horizontal *brise-soleil*, similar to Rudolph's Milam House, recessed into the facades of the east-facing, double-height living room and the parent's bedroom above it. Given that the sun strikes the house with equal if not greater intensity on the west side as on the east, the terraces speak more to Ernest's desire to make it possible to sit in an open-air, covered space on the ocean side of the house. After a late variation showing an L-shaped-in-section living room, with a shallow terrace, the section was resolved in a final variation extending the floor of the now centrally located, single-story living room out to become the floor of a double-height screened porch opening to the east, thereby providing both the living room and the parent's bedroom above it with open-air, covered space and sun shading on the eastern, ocean-facing side of the house.

As it was built, the compact, tower-like, three-level house (twenty-seven feet, four inches tall, with three eight-foot floor levels) has a cruciform-shaped floorplan comprised of a wider volume (three

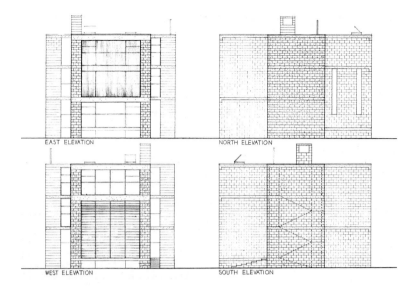

Fig. 3a.4 Ernest House; preliminary elevations.

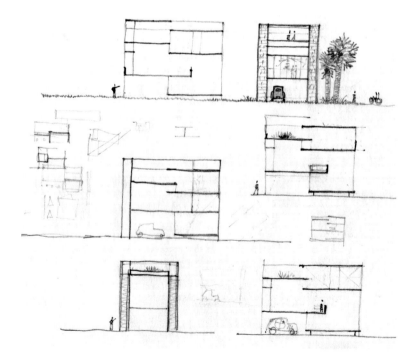

Fig. 3a.5 Ernest House; early east-west section sketches.

ARCHITECTURAL PRACTICE

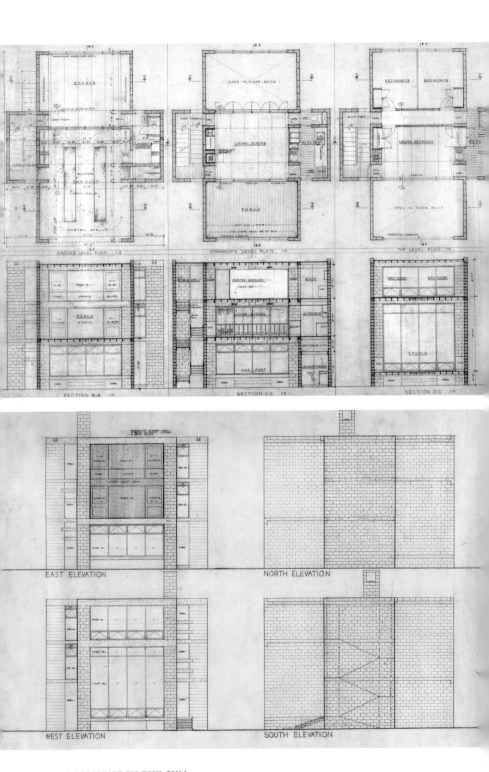

A MOMENT IN THE SUN

twelve-by-twenty-foot spaces) running east-west and a narrower volume (framed by two twelve-by-six-foot spaces) running north-south, and the two volumes interpenetrate at the open, twelve-by-twenty-foot central space of the plan (figs. 3a.6, 3a.7, 3a.8, and 3a.9). The sidewalls on the north and south sides of the house are solid, with no openings, while the east and west walls facing the ocean and garden on the landside, respectively, as well as the interior walls framing the center of the house, are opened to provide light, cross-ventilation, and views to all rooms. The two outer, narrower, twelve-by-six-foot arms of the cruciform plan are set close to the property lines, and house on the north side, the bathroom on the third floor, the kitchen and toilet on the second floor, and the toilet (accessible from the studio by going down four steps), laundry, beach shower, and mechanical on the first floor, and on the south side, the open-air staircase and entry vestibule. The ends of the thickened walls separating the central volumes housing the principal rooms from the peripheral volumes to the north and south are folded to form recesses for storage in the studio, the fireplace, the refrigerator, a vertical duct for the heating and air conditioning, numerous closets, and a dumbwaiter (for groceries and laundry) that serves all three floors, rising from the carport to kitchen to the bath on the bedroom floor.

Though the site is across the road from the row of beachfront houses, views of the ocean to the east and maximum cross-ventilation by prevailing breezes are achieved by elevating the primary rooms of the house. The living/dining room and screened porch are placed on the second floor, the bedrooms on the third floor (the parents' bedroom overlooking the upper part of the screened porch to the ocean view to the east, and the children's bedrooms opening to the west), and the studio closest to ground level for easy access and privacy from the domestic spaces. In accordance with code and good building practice of the time, the studio floor is elevated two feet, eight inches above the ground. In the section of the house as it was built, two double-height, sixteen-foot-tall, twelve-by-twenty-foot rooms, the screened porch on the east side and the studio on the west side, are offset by one level and interlocked so as to allow all three levels of the house to be spatially, visually, and acoustically interconnected. The single-story, twelve-by-twenty-foot living/dining room is centrally located in both plan and section, recessed from the outer edges of the house, and yet has distant views to both the west and the east. The living/dining room overlooks the double-height, glass-walled studio below to the west and is joined to the upper floor bedrooms by the double-height, ocean-side screened porch that opens through sliding

Fig. 3a.6 Ernest House; floorplans and north-south sections through porch, center of tower, and studio; construction drawings.
Fig. 3a.8 Ernest House; elevations; construction drawings.

ARCHITECTURAL PRACTICE

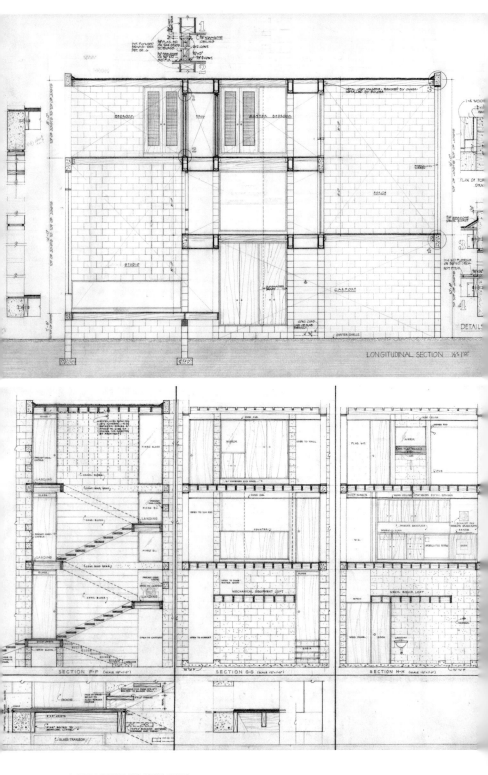

A MOMENT IN THE SUN

glass walls to the east, effectively more than doubling the size of the living/dining room, forming an expansive twenty-four-by-twenty-foot room (figs. 3a.10, 3a.11, 3a.12, 3a.13, 3a.14, and 3a.15).

The windows of all the primary rooms, whether facing outwards or overlooking interior spaces, have both fixed and operable sections, allowing cross-ventilation, daylight penetration, and views. This includes the studio windows opening inwards to the open-air carport to the east, the full-height living room windows opening inwards to the double-height studio to the west (the upper casements of which are equipped with louvered shutters), the full-height, sliding glass wall panels between the living/dining room and the porch, and the parents' bedroom windows opening inwards to the double-height screened porch to the east (each of the four window units comprising three sections that slide down and stack at the bottom). The east-facing windows of the living/dining room and the parents' bedroom are shielded from the low morning sun by being recessed across the twelve-foot depth of the screened porch. The preliminary section drawing submitted to *Progressive Architecture* indicates that Ernest considered equipping the west-facing exterior wall of the studio with a full-height, fixed wood louver system, with glass inserts between the horizontal blades, to break the intense afternoon sunlight (fig. 3a.3). However, as built, the western facade of the studio is made of wood-framed glass, with both fixed and operable window sections, complementing the eastern facade of the screened porch, which is made of wood-framed fiberglass insect screen. Ernest further modified the preliminary design by eliminating the two narrow, vertical, slot-like windows previously shown as being opened in the north wall of the studio, which in the house as built is solid. The west-facing windows in the studio and children's bedrooms above were provided with interior canvas shades that unrolled from the ceiling, allowing each person to adjust them to their liking. Similar shades were installed in the parents' bedroom east-facing windows. The vertical, two-foot, eight-inch-wide, floor-to-ceiling openings to the north and south on all levels of the two service volumes provide, in the north volume, access at the ground floor to the laundry, toilet, and shower, windows in the kitchen and toilet on the second floor, and windows at both ends of the main bath on the third floor, and in the south volume, access and apertures at all levels of the stair.

On the east side of the house, a porous, oyster shell drive leads the short distance from Beach Avenue to the carport, which is set beneath the double-height screened porch and living/dining room on the second floor, and from which the studio can be seen through a glass wall (figs.

Fig. 3a.7 Ernest House; east-west section; construction drawings.
Fig. 3a.9 Ernest House; section through the south tower (left), and sections through the north tower (center and right), construction drawings.

ARCHITECTURAL PRACTICE

Fig. 3a.18 Ernest House; view from guest parking
on Ocean Avenue on west side

Fig. 3a.11 Ernest House; exterior view of eastern porch
and carport facade.

Fig. 3a.12 Ernest House; interior view of double-height porch, looking into living/dining room below and parents' bedroom above; note wall ladder to roof hatch in corner.

Fig. 3a.13 Ernest House; interior view of living/dining room looking towards fireplace at center and onto porch at left. and carport facade.
Fig. 3a.15 Ernest House; interior view of parents' bedroom overlooking porch to right.

A MOMENT IN THE SUN

3a.16, 3a.16a and 3a.17). This view of the house was carefully designed by Ernest in his beautiful eye-level perspective drawing, documenting every concrete block and wood joist, and showing the remarkable degree of visual porosity of the house, with views into all of the rooms (figs. 3a.1 and 3a.11).[28] The accuracy of this drawing is indicated by the evening photograph taken with the house illuminated, in which one can see right through the studio and out into the garden, and where the floor framing, concrete block walls, concrete beams, and wood panel soffits and fascia are highlighted.

Entry for both house guests and studio visitors is from Ocean Boulevard to the west, where is placed the porous, oyster shell-paved off-street parking, from which the more distant view is of the solid mass of the tower house, with the glass facade of the double-height studio and the single-story children's bedrooms above (fig.3a.18, 3a.19). Similar to many early Frank Lloyd Wright buildings, such as the Hardy House (1905) and Unity Temple (1906), there is no opening suggesting the possibility of entry in the center of the front facade; rather one searches for the entry by moving around the side of the main volume. To indicate the approach path, Ernest designed an off-center walkway, originally planned to be made of cylindrical sections of cypress tree trunks, but built of square concrete pavers, which runs along the south edge of the site and leads from the parking across the garden to the entry and staircase on the southern side of the house.

The vertical walls of the house are made entirely of concrete block (finished with silicone sealer) set in a structural (interlocking) running bond, and cast-concrete lintels and bond beams: eight-inch-deep beams marking the floor lines, sixteen-inch-deep lintels at the openings of the studio and screened porch, and sixteen-inch-deep lintel parapets at the roof (figs. 3a.20, 3a.21 and 3a.21a). The two scuppers, allowing rainwater to drain from the roof, are opened on the east sides of the north and south stair and service masses, so as not to be seen from the entry approach. At their outer edges the concrete block walls turn the corner, two courses or thirty-two inches on the central walls and three courses or forty-eight inches on the outer walls, returning to shorten the beam spans and provide lateral stability for wind loads—Jacksonville being prone to hurricanes. While the primary structural materials of locally manufactured concrete block and cast-in-place concrete beams, lintels, bond beams, and foundation are among the most modest and inexpensive available, the craftsmanship exhibited by the builder under Ernest's supervision is exceptional, resulting in flat, taut wall surfaces and crisp, tight corners inside and out (fig. 3a.22).

The wood framing of the floors and roof, exposed to the rooms below, spans between the outer concrete beams, lintels, and bond beams and between the inner pairs of plywood box beams—a then innovative

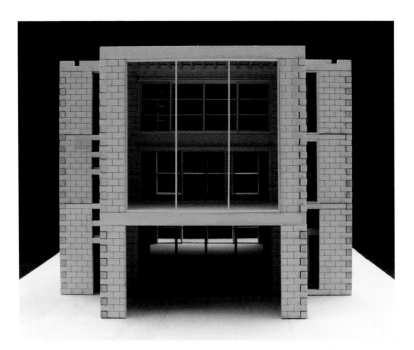

Fig. 3a.16 Ernest House; exterior view of model from northeast,
(model made under author's supervision).
Fig. 3a.17 Ernest House; view of model looking through carport to studio.

ARCHITECTURAL PRACTICE

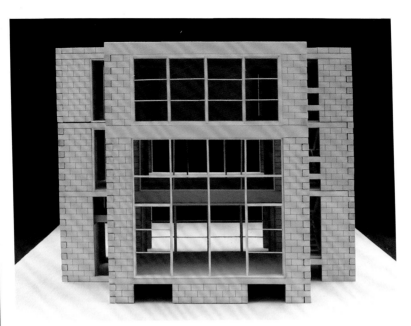

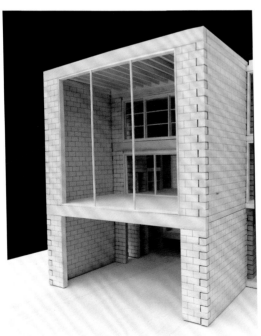

Fig. 3a.19
Ernest House; exterior view
of model from west
(model made under author's
supervision).
Fig. 3a.16a
Ernest House; exterior view
of model from east.

Fig. 3a.10
Ernest House; exterior view
of western studio and entry
facade.

stressed-skin structure that uses the plywood as the diaphragm—at the center of the house, which enclose the mechanical ductwork above plywood soffits, with two openings cut through the plywood box beams to accommodate the air diffusers (fig. 3a.23). The plywood box beams are substituted by concrete lintel-beams at the east and west ends of the floors, including the two shifted floors that stop at the inner edges of the double-height volumes of the porch and studio, and these concrete lintel beams act to tie the concrete block wall bearing structure and block end walls on the north and south to the wood and concrete spanning structure at the center of the house. While very economical to build— the roughly 2,200-square-foot house was built for $10 per square foot in 1961—the house is remarkably resolved in every aspect of its design and construction.

The detailing of the house consistently provides for the use and comfort of the inhabitants, as well as the enrichment of their experience through the way it was built and the way it opens to the environment. Because there are no vertical structural elements in the center of the floor plan, all the rooms are entirely opened to east and west, allowing generous natural light, cross-ventilation, and views. The sole exception is the stained cypress wood privacy wall between the parents' and children's bedrooms on the third floor, and yet even there the door openings are aligned so that during the day cross-ventilation is allowed. The eight-by-sixteen-inch module established by the concrete block fabric of the walls is complemented by the sixteen-inch module of the wood floor framing and by the four-foot (equal to three concrete blocks) module of the vertical wood window mullions and built-in cabinetry throughout the house. The stair is made of wood deck floorboard landings and open wood treads, and a thick, flexible wall of woven sisal fabric is stretched between the landings at the center of the sets of stairs to prevent falls. The U-shaped-in-section concrete bond beams that serve as parapet rails for the stair landings on the east and west are employed as planters, as can be seen in the photograph of Ernest standing on the stair (fig. 3a.24). The screened porch, which like the stair is exposed to the elements, is also given a wood deck floor. The other primary rooms have wall-to-wall sisal carpet, a tough fiber able to withstand sand and salt water. The ground floor landing of the stair and the toilet and laundry rooms have concrete slabs on grade, and on the upper floors the "wet" rooms of kitchen and bath have ceramic tile floors. A particularly telling detail is Ernest's provision of cork floors in the two-foot, eight-inch square vestibule spaces separating the "wet" rooms of the kitchen and bath from the "dry" central living rooms and bedrooms, as well as the similar cork-floor vestibules that separate the weather-exposed stair from the primary central rooms on all floors, including the studio.

Finally, mention should be made of the custom-designed pinwheel table Ernest built for his studio, visible in the view from above (where the Circusland project model and the Jacksonville Youth Center drawing can be seen on the board) (fig. 3a.14) and developed in a series of sketches (fig. 3a.25). The pier-like legs of the square table are set to the corner, and their orientation rotates so that each side has one narrow face of the leg and one wide face of the leg. This innovative arrangement allows for four people (or four project drawings), each with their own drafting straight-edge (called a T-square) hooked to the left table edge, to sit and work at the table at the same time.

The Robert Ernest House was praised in the award issues of both *Progressive Architecture* ("PA Awards") in 1961 and *Architectural Record* ("Record Houses") in 1962 for its simple, economical construction and planning, its multi-level design minimizing the roof and foundation area, its utilization of low-cost materials such as concrete block and wood framing, and its collection of the utilities into the north service tower to minimize piping and venting. It was also praised for its "ingenious interior spatial arrangement"[29] that frees "the interior for a number of open living spaces with a wide variety of sizes and views."[30] In an article published in the July 1962 issue of the American Institute of Architect's (AIA) *Florida Architect* honoring Ernest following his death, Jacksonville architect Robert Broward wrote of the Robert Ernest House: "Built on a narrow lot facing the ocean, of simple materials and at a construction cost of about $22,000, this is a multipurpose as well as multistory building. It combines a studio-office at ground level with living quarters above—and it does so simply, efficiently, and attractively. Use of balancing service towers permits full utilization of interior space."[31] In addition to Ernest's early employment of Kahn's concept of "servant"

Fig. 3a.24
Ernest House; interior view of stair with sisal fabric center wall, concrete bond beams used as planters, and Ernest standing on landing.

ARCHITECTURAL PRACTICE

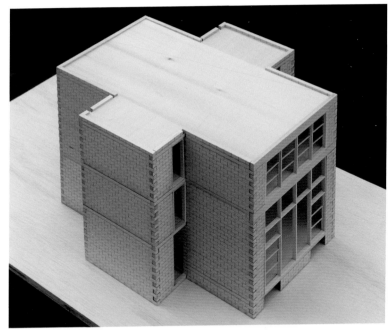

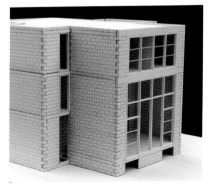

Fig. 3a.20
Ernest House; aerial view of model
from northwest (model made under author's
supervision).
Fig. 3a.21
Ernest House; exterior view of model,
with studio and bedrooms on west side.
Fig. 3a.21a
Ernest House; elevated exterior view
of model from southwest.

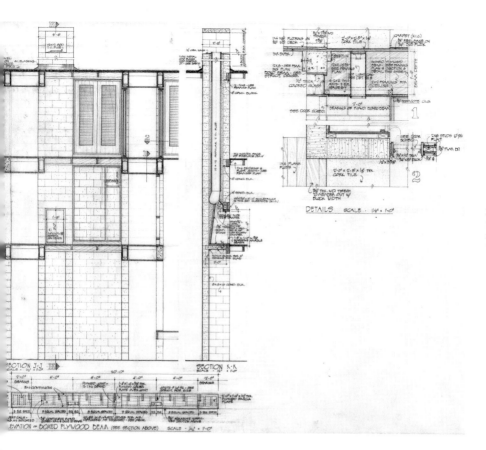

Fig. 3a.23
Ernest House;
section through the
center of the house,
with detail of box-beams
housing mechanical
(below) and section
of fireplace (right).

Fig. 3a.25
Ernest House;
Ernest sketches
for studio drawing table.

Fig. 3a.22
Ernest House; exterior
view of west side
of stair tower.

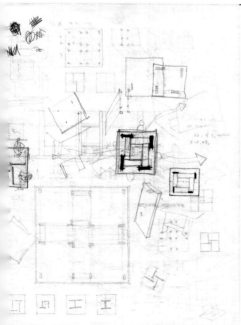

ARCHITECTURAL PRACTICE

and "served" space in the stair and service towers, we should also note the sustainability of the cross-ventilation of all spaces and the absence of impervious surfaces on the site, including beneath the house, allowing rainwater to percolate. This ingenious house, in which Ernest lived and worked for only a little more than one year, is at once economical and yet experientially enriching, energy conserving and yet environmentally engaging, modest and yet monumental.

Eli Becker House, Jacksonville, Florida, 1960-61

At the same time that he was working on his own home and studio, Ernest designed and supervised the construction of the Eli Becker House on a site opening onto the Arlington River, a tributary of the St. John's River, in Jacksonville. In its spatial order and engagement of its site, the Eli Becker House could not be more different from the Robert Ernest House, indicating the remarkable range of the twenty-seven-year-old architect. The Eli Becker House is sited at the center of a long, narrow wooded 100-by-474-foot lot that runs from Clifton Road at its north end to the shore of the Arlington River at its south end, sloping a total of twelve feet from the north to the south. Unlike the vertical, three-story Robert Ernest House, the Eli Becker House is built on a single ground floor, and it extends and unfolds horizontally to anchor itself to, and engage with, its expansive, gently sloping site.

The house has a highly resolved hexagonal plan composition of equilateral triangles, sixteen feet on each side—a return to one of Ernest's favorite ordering geometries, and another difference from the rectangular geometry of the Ernest House (figs. 3b.1, 3b.2, 3b.3, and 3b.4). The triangular sections are clustered in an irregular U-shaped plan to form an entry court at the center, with a large, hexagonal carport opening off the kitchen at the north end and a hexagonal swimming pool opening off the living room at the south end (fig. 3b.5). A series of masonry-walled, hexagonal service towers and hexagonal columns, centered on the intersections of the sixteen-foot equilateral triangular grid, anchor the continuously flowing interior spaces. The serrated perimeter of the house alternately folds inwards and unfurls outwards, interlocking the house with the surrounding live oak trees, sloping landscape, and riverfront (fig. 3b.6).

The code-required, 200-foot setback from the river determined the southernmost interior space of the house, with only the swimming pool and its terrace extending closer to the river (fig. 3b.7). As a result, the house was located near the midpoint of the site, where the largely flat northern half of the site meets the gently sloping southern half. In plan, the house extends seventy feet between the fifteen-foot setbacks from the property lines to the east and west, with the short, solid walls facing the neighboring houses on either side providing privacy for the family. The house is approached on a porous, oyster shell driveway that begins

Fig. 3b.1 Eli Becker House, Arlington River, Jacksonville, Florida, 1960–61; aerial exterior view of model from east (model made under author's supervision).

at the corner of Clifton and Sandra Roads, passes the hexagonal concrete block-walled trashcan enclosure (designed by Ernest as a hint of what is to come), and bends to the south, where the oyster shell parking area for guests fronts onto the two openings of the large hexagonal carport. Although the carport is labeled "garage" on the drawings, not being enclosed, it is better described as a carport, the term Ernest used for a similar space in his own house. In daily use, the carport forms a front porch for the residents, as one can enter directly to the kitchen, allowing for covered access in all weathers. The front door of the house is accessed by walking around the west side of the carport to reach the intimately scaled hexagonal entry court, which is framed by the solid, vertical concrete block walls of two of the larger service towers, with large windows opening into the kitchen and study on either side, and the front door in the center (figs. 3b.8 and 3b.9).

The entry is housed in one of the smaller hexagonal towers, with three solid sides and three open sides. Across from the front door, two openings lead to the kitchen and dining room on the left and to the living

Fig. 3b.4 Becker House; aerial plan view of model with house roofs removed (model made under author's supervision).

Fig. 3b.3 Becker House; aerial exterior view of model from northwest, with entry court
Fig. 3b.2 Becker House; aerial exterior view of model from south

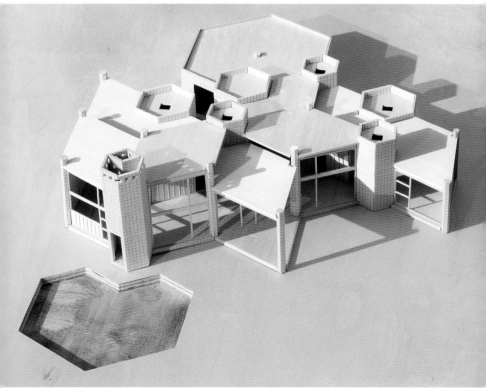

ARCHITECTURAL PRACTICE

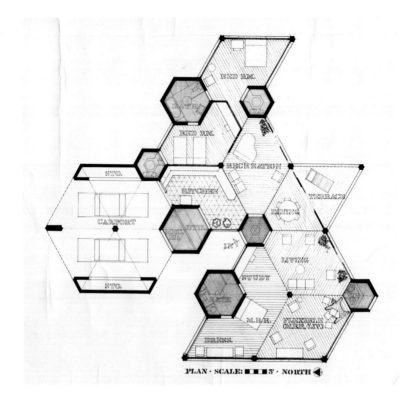

PLAN · SCALE: ■■■ 5′ · NORTH ◀

Fig. 3b.5 Becker House; floorplan.

Fig. 3b.7 Becker House; site plan, construction drawings.

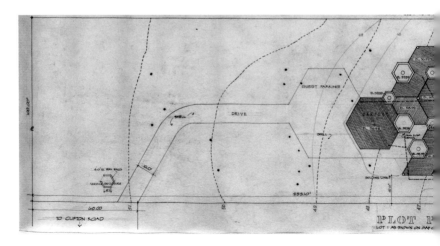

A MOMENT IN THE SUN

Fig. 3b.6 Becker House; preliminary perspective view from southeast, without pool and terrace.

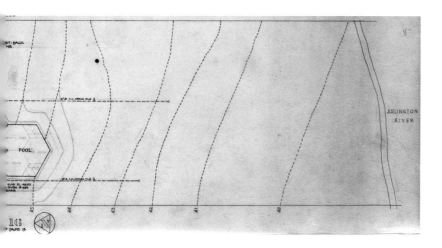

A MOMENT IN THE SUN

Fig. 3b.8 Becker House; interior view from living room, looking east-northeast, with entry (left), porch (right), dining room, and bedroom door (center).

Fig. 3b.9 Becker House; view of exterior from the northwest, carport behind trees to left, and entry court at center.

Fig. 3b.10 Becker House; view of entry court.

ARCHITECTURAL PRACTICE

room on the right (figs. 3b.10 and 3b.11). These two rhombus-in-plan spaces, each comprised of two of the sixteen-foot-sided triangles, have the two highest ceilings in the house, the living room being the higher of the two, and are separated and connected by a triangular space with a lower ceiling that extends through the glass wall to cover the triangular exterior porch (fig. 3b.12). The rhombus-in-plan kitchen wraps around the large hexagonal tower containing the utilities and mechanical equipment. It has windows onto the entry court and carport and is open to the dining room (fig.3b.13). The ceiling of the kitchen is the same height as the space between the living and dining rooms. The carport is the largest and most geometrically regular space in the house, comprising six of the sixteen-foot-sided triangles arranged to form a hexagonal space, with solid-walled storage closets to the north and south, and is given the lowest ceiling (fig.3b.14).

Beyond the dining room to the east are two bedrooms, with the lowest ceilings in the house (matching that of the carport), which share a large hexagonal tower housing the bath, and each of which have a closet in a small hexagonal tower. Beyond the living room is a rhombus-in-plan space, labelled "flexible" on the plans, opening to the living room and the main bedroom, and which is anchored at its southern 120-degree corner by the dual-opening fireplace housed in a smaller hexagonal tower. The main bedroom is a large room, comprised of three sixteen-foot-sided triangles, and it's ceiling is at the same height as that of the dining room. The main bedroom wraps around the large hexagonal tower containing the bath (with a hexagonal, ceramic-tile bathtub sunk into the floor), has high windows opening on either side to the entry court to the north, and has built-in closet and cabinets along the entire length of the solid, thirty-two-foot west wall of the house (fig. 3b.15). On the final construction drawings, Ernest showed a set of folding walls that can be used to close off the main bedroom and flexible space from the living room (thus the dual openings in the fireplace for living room and bedroom), but these walls were not built. As a result, the living room, dining room, flexible space, and main bedroom, comprising ten of the sixteen, sixteen-foot-sided triangles in the interior of the house, is experienced as one continuously flowing space (fig. 3b.16).

Outside of the living room and flexible space, the hexagonal swimming pool extends to the south towards the riverfront and is surrounded by an extension of the concrete terrace originating in the covered space across from the entry (fig. 3b.17). In the early study model, and in the first iteration of the construction drawings, Ernest proposed that the swimming pool be composed of three connected hexagons, each with

Fig. 3b.11 Becker House; interior view from dining room, looking west-southwest, with to entry (right), living room, and multipurpose room (center).

Fig. 3b.12 Becker House; interior view from living room, looking west, with dining room (left), and porch and view to riverfront (center right).
Fig. 3b.14 Becker House; interior view of carport, looking west.

Fig. 3b.15 Becker House; interior view from dressing room and bedroom, looking south to multipurpose room and fireplace.
Fig. 3b.13 Becker House; interior view of kitchen, looking south to entry (right) and dining room.

Fig. 3b.16 Becker House; interior view from dining room, looking west-southwest, with entry (right), pool (left), and multipurpose room (center).

A MOMENT IN THE SUN

ARCHITECTURAL PRACTICE

Fig. 3b.17 Becker House; exterior view looking north, with pool, terrace, and porch.

Fig. 3b.18 Becker House; exterior view looking east-northeast, with concrete block tower containing shower outside and fireplace inside.

a different water depth.[32] The swimming pool and its narrow terrace deck wraps around the smaller hexagonal tower housing the fireplace inside and a shower outside (fig. 3b.18). Above the shower, an open slat-roof grille is recessed two feet, eight inches below the top of the fireplace tower, forming a turret-like space. In an intriguing detail, Ernest removed every other concrete block from the row just below the top of the fireplace tower, creating a series of square openings, through some of which the sky can be seen at the crown of this, the tallest tower in the house. This detail does not appear either in the final elevations on the construction drawings or in the detail section of the fireplace, and thus was a decision Ernest made during the construction of the house.

The folding south facade of the house, overlooking the river, is, with the exception of the two hexagonal towers, entirely glazed (or open, beneath the triangular terrace roof), as depicted in Ernest's perspective rendering (fig. 3b.6, 3b.19, and 3b.20). As the house unfolds from east to west across the site, the width of the interior spaces varies from a minimum of sixteen feet to a maximum of thirty-two feet, with full-height windows opening to the south and smaller windows opening to the north, so that the interior is continuously flooded with daylight, provided good cross-ventilation, as well as enjoying expansive views to the river. As can be seen in the site plan, the folding and staggering southern facade of the house roughly parallels the angle of the river shoreline, further anchoring the house to its place (fig. 3b.7).

The Eli Becker House was constructed using many of the same methods developed by Frank Lloyd Wright in building his Usonian houses starting in the 1930s, most notably in the inscribing of the planning grid of the house into the concrete floor slab. The floor of the Eli Becker House is formed of equilateral sixteen-foot triangular sections of concrete slab on grade. In the construction drawings, Ernest provided "Layout Diagrams" for the concrete foundations and concrete floor slab, showing how the equilateral triangles and their meeting points were to be inscribed into the floor (fig. 3b.21). This effectively mitigated the need for dimension strings running across the plan, as the contractor only needed to measure to the nearest triangular edge or meeting point marked in the concrete floor slab. The structural walls and columns of the house are constructed of custom precast rhombus-shaped concrete blocks, with 60- and 120-degree corners, eight inches square on each side, which are nested in sets of three to form the hexagonal columns (fig. 3b.22).[33] The rhombus-shaped concrete blocks indicate both Ernest's constructive ingenuity, documented in the photographs of the various stacking patterns possible, and the fact that at this time in Florida concrete blocks were manufactured locally and, if desired, could be custom precast in architect-designed metal forms at no additional cost, as was done in this case by David Concrete Products in Jacksonville. Due to their square-finished faces, when the rhombus-shaped blocks were set in a structurally interlocking running bond, where each alternating layer of blocks overlaps its neighbors below and above (all tied together by vertical reinforcing steel bars threaded through the voids at the centers of the concrete blocks), the concrete block walls nevertheless presented a perfect square grid, the same appearance they would have if set in a nonstructural stack bond.

On the construction drawings, Ernest also provided diagrams of the repeating typical conditions of the the large and small hexagon towers and the hexagonal columns (eight inches on a side), thus eliminating the need to repeat these details in the floorplan (fig. 3b.21). The solid-walled

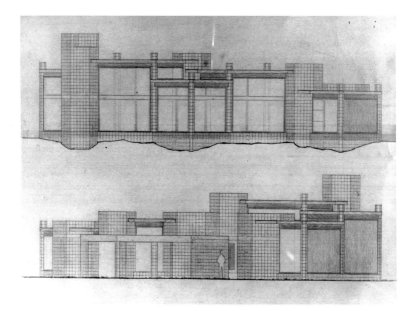

Fig. 3b.19 Becker House; largely open south elevation (above), largely closed north elevation (below).

Fig. 3b.20 Becker House; exterior view of house, looking west-northwest.

ARCHITECTURAL PRACTICE

Fig. 3b.22 Becker House; series of photographs of rhombus-shaped concrete block mock-ups, showing its use in column and wall construction.

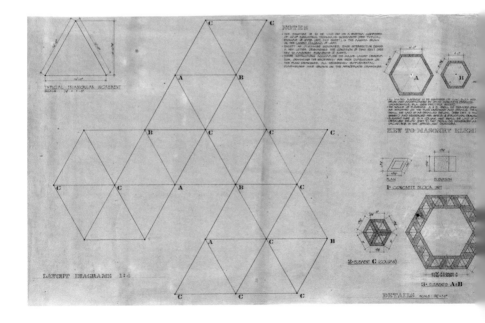

Fig. 3b.21 Becker House; "diagrams" showing geometry of house and concrete block setting patterns, construction drawings.

A MOMENT IN THE SUN

service spaces are housed in three larger hexagonal towers, six feet on each exterior side and ten feet across on the inside, containing bathrooms, utilities, and mechanical, and four smaller hexagonal towers, four feet on each exterior side and six feet across on the inside, containing the closets, fireplace, and entry. The hexagonal towers and the hexagonal columns bear on perimeter and point footings and are tied together by concrete edge and bond beams at six-foot, eight-inches above the floor. Skylights are opened in the roofs of all the hexagonal towers housing the entry, bathrooms, and closets (except those housing the fireplace and mechanical), and two skylights are opened in the kitchen ceiling, centered on the two triangles in its plan.

Above each of the sixteen-foot-sided triangular sections of concrete floor slab are matching triangular wood-framed roof sections, which are supported by three ten-inch-deep laminated wood beams that frame the outer edges, and which bear on the hexagonal masonry towers and hexagonal columns (fig. 3b.23). The triangular roof sections are set at varying heights in two-foot increments from eight to fourteen feet, and the interior edges of each roof section are offset from adjacent roof sections by a minimum of two feet (fig. 3b.24). In the interior rooms of the house,

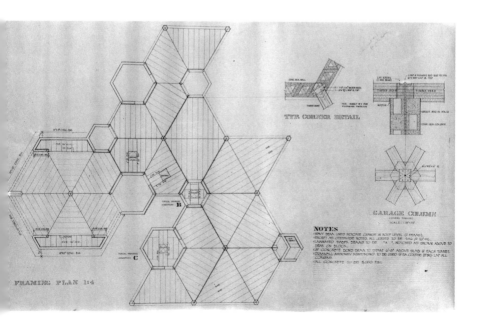

Fig. 3b.23 Becker House; roof-framing plan and details, construction drawings.

the roof framing of six-inch-deep wood joists running between the ten-inch-deep wood edge beams was filled with fiberglass wool insulation and covered by the one-inch-thick refrigeration cork ceiling panels, set in a running bond overlapping pattern and providing additional insulation. The rhombus-in-plan ceiling sections above the living room, dining room, and flexible space are divided by the projecting base of the wood beams that mark the joints between the two, sixteen-foot-sided triangles of which they are comprised. As we move through the house, the triangular roof sections are constantly moving up and down with respect to each other, and the joints between each roof section are articulated during the day by bands of clerestory windows varying from six inches to two feet, six inches in height and during the night by recessed uplighting set beneath each window (fig. 3b.25).

The nonstructural walls of the house are made of two-by-four-inch wood structural studs with plywood sheathing, insulation, and are faced inside and out with vertical, wide wood boards with vertical, narrow wood battens applied over their joints (called "board-and-batten"). The fixed and operable windows are wood-framed, the glass sliding doors are aluminum-framed, and all apertures are trimmed in wood. The primary rooms of the house have floors of sisal fiber carpeting set over resilient base on the concrete slabs, the entry and two baths in the hexagonal towers have hexagonal ceramic tile floors, and the kitchen has a sheet vinyl floor. Ernest's desire to expose the structure at the ceilings meant there could be no chase spaces for the mechanical ducts. Instead, he and his mechanical engineer designed a network of air ducts cast in concrete beneath the floor slab of the house, through which air-conditioning and heating was distributed from the mechanical space at the carport to the rooms above through floor diffusers. The varying-sized cylindrical sheet metal "under-slab ducts" were cast below the four-inch concrete floor slab, with three inches of concrete surrounding the sides and bottom of each duct, and with the vapor barrier under the floor slab following bottom of duct curve.

The roof framing is only exposed to the space below at the uninsulated carport, where the joists of the six, sixteen-foot-sided sections run parallel to the outside edges, and between the six laminated wood beams that radiate from the hexagonal column at the center, where the six laminated beams are mitered to 60-degree points meeting at the center of

Fig. 3b.24 Becker House; composite section with details of stepping roof and beams, construction drawings.

Fig. 3b.25 Becker House; interior view of intersection of several roof levels, with concrete block columns, clerestory windows, wood beams and recessed uplighting trays, cork ceiling, and board-and-batten wood wall panels.

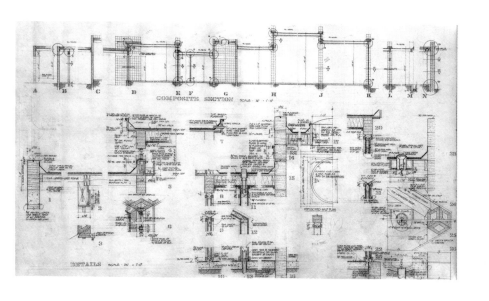

the column (fig. 3b.14). This constructional tour de force at the roof of the carport, rather than being the exception, is the rule in this house, and the construction drawings contain several sheets of section and plan details for how the builder was to secure the laminated wood beams and wood-framed walls, as well as the windows, doors, and wood trim, to the 120-degree corners of the concrete block walls and columns (fig. 3b.24) The result is the rich material dialogue experienced when inhabiting the house, with the complementary pairing of natural cork ceiling above and sisal fiber floor below, the contrasting pairing of vertical concrete block tower walls and vertical wood board-and-batten walls opened with wood-framed windows, and the integrative deployment of wood framing and trim throughout to articulate the joints between the materials (fig. 3b.16). This attention to the integration of materials through its detailing extended to the extensive built-in cabinetry at the kitchen, bedrooms, and living room, and even included Ernest's apparently never-executed designs for triangular plywood chairs. Despite all their differences, what connects the Robert Ernest House and the Eli Becker House is the remarkable level of resolution in their spatial order and in the tectonic clarity of their construction, and how these together enrich the experience of their inhabitants.

In July 1962 Robert Broward wrote of the Eli Becker House: "This building, one of the few completed during Robert Ernest's independent professional practice, embodies more than a mere unconventional approach to the solution of a residential design problem. It clearly indicates a firm understanding of Florida living needs and the ability to provide unique spatial answers to them. More importantly, however, it suggests the depth of three-dimensional thinking, the appreciation of orderly structure, and the sensitivity to the value of form, texture and color that characterizes the work of this young architect—and gave a basic promise of brilliant things to come."[34] While the hexagonal plan of the Eli Becker House is likely inspired by the similar geometries of Frank Lloyd Wright's much-publicized hexagonal-grid plan Usonian houses such as the Hana House (1936), which was built of rectangular brick, a much closer and more intriguing parallel can be drawn to Wright's almost-contemporary Stromquist House (1958), which, like the Eli Becker House, employed rhombus-shaped concrete blocks. At the same time, due to the powerfully spatial and structural deployment of the hexagonal towers, and the clear rhythm of servant and served spaces that results, as well as in the careful revelation of all the materials of construction, in experience the Eli Becker House has a far stronger relation to the buildings of Louis Kahn.

Among several of Ernest's projects that were moving toward construction at the time of his death, but which remained unrealized, was the library addition to the Bartram School, a girls' school founded in 1934 (which Ernest's wife Lynwood attended), located off Bartram Road to the southeast of downtown Jacksonville, and opening to Little Pottsburg Creek on the east side of the St. John's River. The two-story library was set to the north of the existing buildings, to which it was attached by a narrow, covered walkway, with two existing large live oak trees between. The first scheme is a north-south, double-square in plan with two open-air stairs anchoring the corners of the south end, a central library and study hall on the ground floor, and three central classrooms and a projection room on the upper floor (figs. 3c.1 and 3c.2). A deep, open-air covered balcony on the east and west sides, structured by large piers, surrounds the library and classrooms on both levels, and the first elevations show a series of semi-circular arches at the top of the piers.

The second scheme for the Bartram School has a similar plan configuration to the first scheme but does not carry the arched piers forward. The two staircases, framed by solid sidewalls, are pivoted out to east and west, demarcating the "head" of the building to the south, with the large, thirty-by-forty-foot, open-air, covered entry porch on the ground floor and the bedrooms for faculty and students on the upper floor (a new component of the program in this phase of design), from the larger "body" of the building to the north (figs. 3c.3 and 3c.4). The central, twenty-seven-by-fifty-four-foot, double square-in-plan library on the ground floor and three classrooms on the upper floor are framed and shaded on the east and west by deep, open-air, covered balconies. The balconies are set behind full-building-height brick piers projecting to the east and west (similar to the staircases), which extend from the ground to the concrete edge beam at the roof (similar to Ernest's design for the convent in New Orleans) (fig. 3c.5). The piers form five ten-foot bays between the staircases and the large study hall on the ground floor and the projection room on the upper floor that extend across the north end of the building. A freestanding central fireplace anchors the north end of the taller library and joins it to the study hall to form a large, T-shaped space. Despite being recessed behind porches on three sides, the library is generously illuminated by three ten-foot-wide, glazed entries on the south, east, and west, as well as by large clerestory windows opened above the bookcases on the east and west walls. This final design is considerably more resolved than the first scheme in the integration of its formal language, in the articulation of the tectonic elements of walls and piers, and in its deployment of the servant and served spaces.

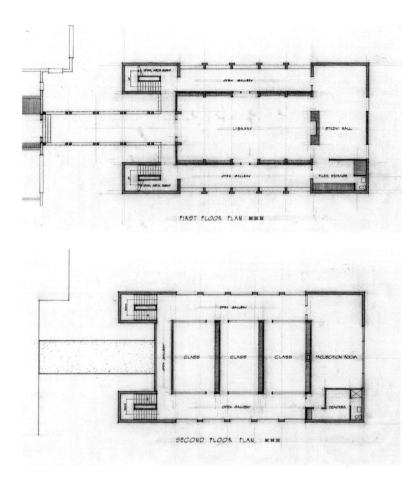

FIRST FLOOR PLAN ■■■

SECOND FLOOR PLAN ■■■

Fig. 3c.1 Bartram School Library Addition, Jacksonville, Florida (project); first scheme, first-floor plan (north to right).
Fig. 3c.2 Bartram School Library; first scheme, second-floor plan.

Fig. 3c.3 Bartram School Library; second scheme, first-floor plan.
Fig. 3c.4 Bartram School Library, second scheme, second-floor plan.
Fig. 3c.5 Bartram School Library; second scheme, east elevation (above left), south elevation (above right), transverse section (below left), and north elevation (below right).

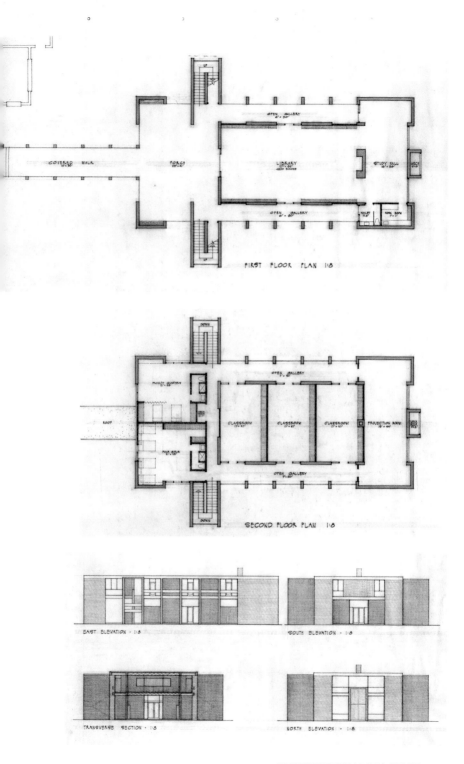

FIRST FLOOR PLAN 1:8

SECOND FLOOR PLAN 1:8

EAST ELEVATION · 1:8

SOUTH ELEVATION · 1:8

TRANSVERSE SECTION · 1:8

NORTH ELEVATION · 1:8

ARCHITECTURAL PRACTICE

Robert and Martha Read House, Jacksonville, Florida (project)

The Robert and Martha Read House, designed for a small, 115-foot-deep, 65-foot-wide lot in the Venetia neighborhood of Jacksonville on the west side of the St. John's River and north of the Naval Air Station, was scheduled to be constructed in early 1961. A full set of construction drawings and specifications were prepared for the house, indicating that construction was imminent. The site is in the second row of houses off the riverfront to the east and runs between Venetia Boulevard to the east, onto which the house fronted, and Roma Boulevard to the west, off of which the carport opened. All the rooms of the one-story house (except the covered carport) are organized within a sixty-six-by-forty-nine-foot rectangular plan, with narrow, eight-foot setbacks from the property lines to north and south, and twenty-five-foot setbacks from the streets to the east and west (figs. 3d.1, 3d.2, and 3d.3). The house plan is organized around a central courtyard, with a glazed hallway separating the central courtyard from a second courtyard to the west, which opens to the carport.

The shared rooms are set along the north and east side of the house, with the living room at the center of the east elevation, opened through sliding glass doors to a covered terrace off the central courtyard, the dining room at the northeast corner, and the kitchen and family room at the center of the north side, with mechanical and laundry to the west, adjacent to the carport. The living room, kitchen, and family room open onto the central courtyard, where the massive double fireplace, which opens into the family room inside and the central courtyard outside, anchors the entire house. In the central courtyard, a ladder next to the fireplace gives access to the roof terrace, which would have provided views of the river. The bedrooms are all set along the south and east side of the house, with the guest room to the east, children's subdividable bedroom in the center, and larger parents' bedroom to the west.

The living room, kitchen, family room, and bedroom hallway open onto the central courtyard, while the parents' bedroom opens onto the second courtyard, providing generous light and cross-ventilation. The majority of the house has a flat roof, but three of the rooms have upward-sloping roofs and clerestory windows, with that of the living room, the tallest, opening to the west, that of the children's bedroom opening to the north, and that of the parents' bedroom opening to the north, where it combines with the sliding glass doors onto the second western courtyard to make a full-height glazed wall. As a result of the glass-walled courtyards and roof clerestory windows, despite the close

Fig. 3d.1 Robert and Martha Read House, Jacksonville, Florida (project); floorplan, construction drawings.
Fig. 3d.3 Read House; sections, courtyard elevations and details, construction drawings.

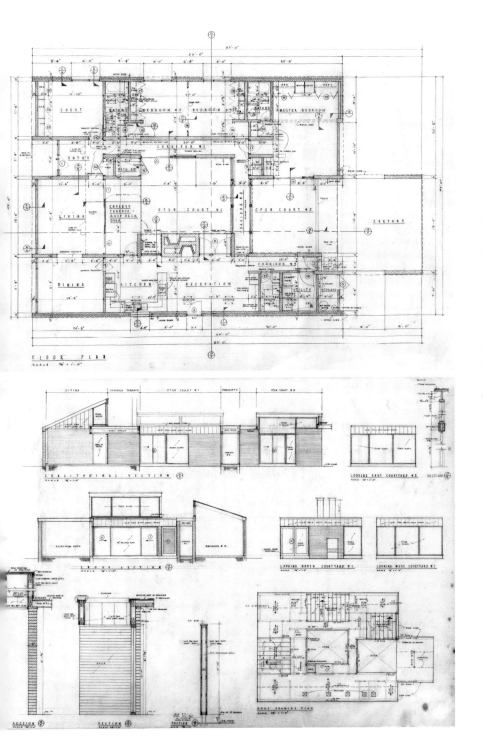

ARCHITECTURAL PRACTICE

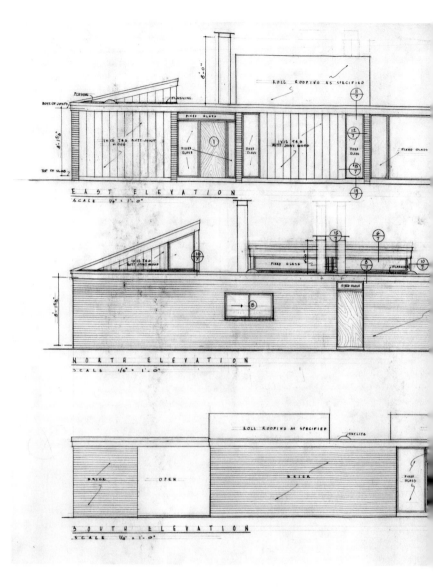

Fig. 3d.2 Read House; elevations, construction drawings.

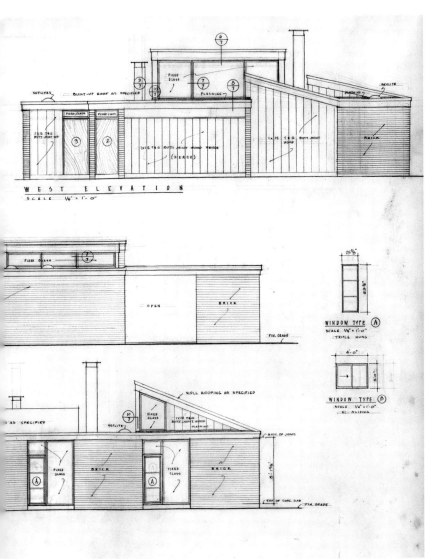

WEST ELEVATION
SCALE 1/4" = 1'-0"

WINDOW TYPE Ⓐ
SCALE 1/4" = 1'-0"
TRIPLE HUNG

WINDOW TYPE Ⓑ
SCALE 1/4" = 1'-0"
AL. SLIDING

ARCHITECTURAL PRACTICE

proximity of the neighboring houses and streets, all but two of the rooms receive light from more than one direction without sacrificing privacy. Circulation takes place around the central courtyard, forming a pinwheel with the entry and bedroom hallways along the south side, the living and dining rooms along the east side, the kitchen, family room, and carport along the north side, and the family room connecting to the bedroom wing across the glazed hallways between the courtyards.

The house is structured by a series of brick bearing walls running east to west, with a concrete floor slab on grade and a wood-framed roof. The three interior brick bearing walls are shifted only once, in order to allow the central courtyard and its corridor to reach across the entire middle section of the plan. Parallel to the interior brick bearing walls on the exterior, brick cavity (double-layered) bearing walls run along the north and south sides of the house, with one-by-twelve-inch vertical, tongue-and-groove wood siding cladding the wood stud–framed east and west exterior walls. The Read House is a contemporary interpretation of the traditional courtyard house type, which provides spatial variety, extensive daylight, cross-ventilation, and privacy in urbanized areas by opening courtyards within the house, effectively expanding the footprint of the house to fill its site, rather than treating the house as a freestanding object surrounded on all sides by a lawn and set within a suburban landscape.

Albert Jr. and Donna Ernest House, Jacksonville, Florida (project)

Ernest's design for a house for his brother Albert Jr., his wife Donna, and their family, which was not realized, was sited on a 200-acre riverfront lot on the west side of the St. John's River in Orange Park, a suburb south of downtown Jacksonville. The final scheme (July 1961) is rigorously ordered in plan, using a tartan grid of Palladian whole-number bay rhythm proportions, while having a relaxed, almost informal quality in section. The two-story house is entered from the west and opens to the east, towards the nearby river, and the two primary facades are symmetrical (figs. 3e.1, 3e.2, 3e.3, and 3e.4). The thirty-six-by-forty-four-foot ground floorplan has a long shallow entry porch, with doors to the maid's room and den at its two ends, and the glass-walled entry into the foyer and stair hall at the center. In the middle of the plan, a lateral passage linking the three primary rooms of the house—living room, dining room, and family room—is terminated by a pair of massive eight-foot-wide rubble stone fireplaces that project beyond the exterior walls of the house and anchor the living room to the north and the kitchen to the south. Here Ernest shows his mastery of plan-making by using the lateral passage to seamlessly shift the planning grid from the five-bay tartan grid (ten feet, six feet, twelve feet, six feet, ten feet) of the west, entry side, to the three-bay centered grid (fourteen feet, sixteen feet, fourteen feet)

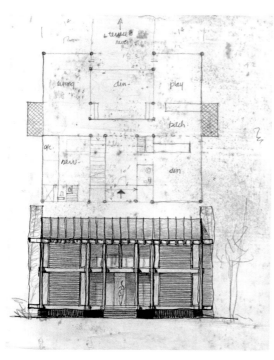

Fig. 3e.1 Albert Jr. and Donna
Ernest House, Jacksonville, Florida (project);
preliminary floorplan and west (entry and landside)
elevation.
Fig. 3e.6 A. and D. Ernest House; north elevation.
Fig. 3e.4 A. and D. Ernest House; east (waterfront) elevation, with diagram of floorplan and
perspective sketch of house seen from river.
Fig. 3e.5 A. and D. Ernest House; transverse
section.

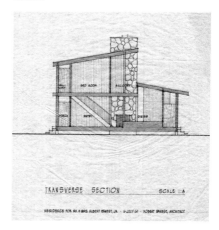

TRANSVERSE SECTION   SCALE 1:8

RESIDENCE FOR MR. & MRS. ALBERT ERNEST, JR. · 9 JULY '64 · ROBERT BROOST, ARCHITECT

ARCHITECTURAL PRACTICE

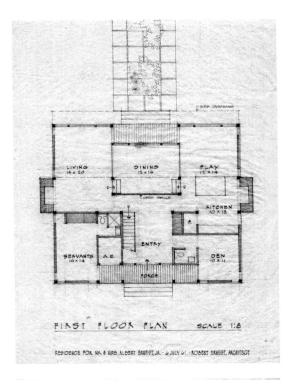

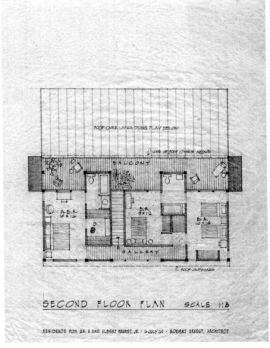

Fig. 3e.2 A. and D. Ernest House; first-floor plan.
Fig. 3e.3 A. and D. Ernest House; second-floor plan.

A MOMENT IN THE SUN

on the east, riverfront side. The staircase rises along the north wall of the foyer to reach the three upper-floor bedrooms, which are accessed by the glass-walled gallery above the entry porch. The three bedrooms share the deep covered balcony—subtly divided into three sections, one for each bedroom, by the two projecting bathroom blocks—which extends between the massive stone chimneys of the twin fireplaces and overlooks the river to the east.

The west-east, transverse section of the house, from entry side to riverside, is covered by two mono-pitch roofs, two-story and one-story, respectively, both of which rise towards the center of the house, their inner edges aligning at the east faces of the fireplaces (figs. 3e.5 and 3e.6). The higher and larger roof over the two-story portion of the house slopes upwards from eight feet over the gallery to twelve feet over the upper balcony, so the views from the bedrooms and balcony open up towards the sky. The lower and smaller roof over living, dining, and family rooms slopes down from twelve feet at the fireplaces to ten feet at the glazed east-facing walls, so the views from the three daytime rooms open out to the horizon and down towards the shoreline of the river. The dining room, elevated two feet above the other rooms on the ground floor and recessed behind a shallow riverfront porch, provides seated eye-level views that match those at standing eye-level in the living and family rooms. This difference in height also constructs a theatrical relationship between the rooms, where the dining room is the elevated "stage" for the foyer (from which it is separated by a vertical wood slat screen), the living room, and the family room (onto both of which it opens directly), on three sides, similar to the early modern houses designed by Adolf Loos.

Square wood columns provide the primary structure for the house, with wood-framed floors and roofs. The wood-stud-framed walls in between the columns are clad with vertical wood boards on the interior, and horizontal wood board siding on the exterior, and the roofs are clad in standing seam metal-roofing. The wood-framed walls are spaced away from the columns and fireplaces by narrow floor-to-ceiling windows. The wood-framed walls, floors, and roofs are disengaged from the two massive rubble-stone fireplaces, which are set outside the perimeter of the house so as to minimize the risk of fire. While exhibiting an informal, relaxed character and employing vernacular roof shapes and construction materials, the plan of the house is rigorously resolved in its plan geometry and employs vertical slots of glass to separate structural from nonstructural elements, and to separate differing materials from each other—all of which are ways of building to be found in the works of both Wright and Kahn.

Circusland Shopping Center, Tampa, Florida (project)

Ernest's largest unrealized project was for the Circusland Shopping Center, which was located on a large site to the south of the approach to the Howard Frankland Bridge, on the shore of Old Tampa Bay in southwest Tampa, Florida. The shopping center was planned in parallel with an amusement park called Circusland, which was to be sited on the waterfront to the west of the shopping center. The client for the project was Maurice Albert, the developer of the Regency Square regional shopping center in the Arlington neighborhood of east Jacksonville (fig. 3f.1).

The shopping center has an irregular, C-shaped plan that follows the perimeter of the twenty-four hexagonal-in-plan, steel truss-framed roof canopies that cover the building (figs. 3f.2 and 3f.3). Each hexagonal roof canopy is sixty-nine feet across and supported at its center by a six-foot-wide, hollow, hexagonal concrete pier, from which it is cantilevered. In section, each hexagonal roof canopy tapers from ten feet deep at the central pier to two feet at the outer edges, forming an upward-sloping ceiling inside and a downward-sloping roof outside. The non-load-bearing curtain walls enclosing the building are hung from the perimeters of the cantilevered canopy trusses. With the exception of three taller sections at the entry, the concrete piers are twenty-seven feet tall, and the ceiling formed by the hexagonal canopies slopes upwards from twelve feet at the pier to sixteen feet at the outer edge.

Entry to the shopping center is from the northeast, through the court formed by the C-shaped plan and beneath the three taller roof canopies, the ceilings of which slope upwards from twenty-two to twenty-six feet—ten feet taller than the ceilings of the typical roof canopies (fig. 3f.4). Once inside the shopping center, the space would have been completely flexible as to how it could be subdivided, and the only vertical structures are the six-foot-wide hexagonal concrete piers, set sixty-nine feet apart. As part of the overall site plan, Ernest also proposed a restaurant to be sited offshore and in the marina to the south of the shopping center, accessed by a walkway, and the restaurant is formed by three of the same sixty-nine-foot-wide hexagonal roof canopies, supported on three hexagonal piers.

Hexagonal-plan roof canopies and structure was an idea that Ernest returned to a number of times in his brief career, beginning with his thesis at University of Virginia, continuing with the underground restaurant he designed while at Yale, and most recently in the carport of the Eli Becker House, where the hexagonal concrete block pier at the center supports six triangular roof sections. But with this project for the Circusland Shopping Center, Ernest brings this concept to a remarkable level of resolution, in both its economy, in its efficient use of minimal and inexpensive materials to enclose maximal space, and its design

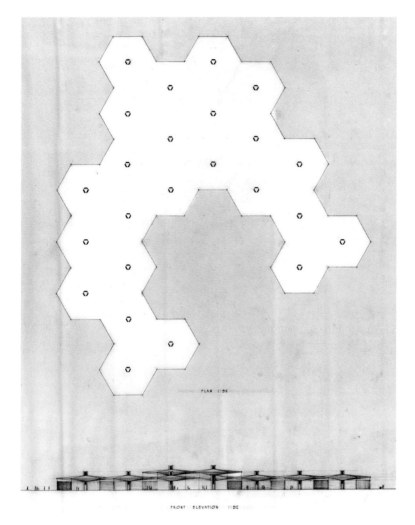

Fig. 3f.2 Circusland Shopping Center; floorplan and front elevation.

ARCHITECTURAL PRACTICE

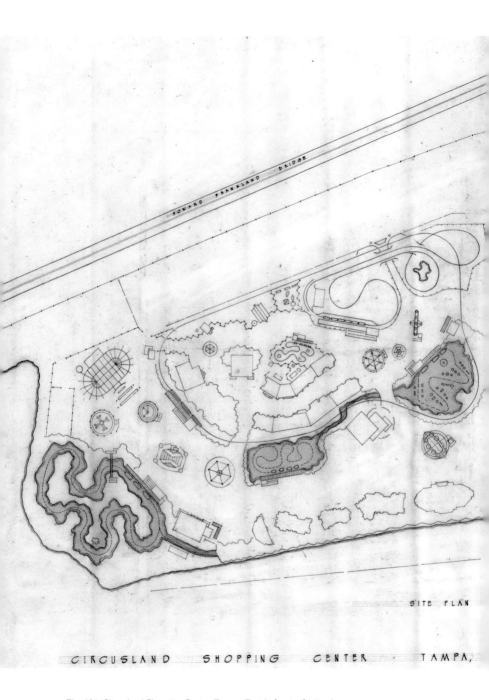

Fig. 3f.1 Circusland Shopping Center, Tampa, Florida (project); site plan.

A MOMENT IN THE SUN

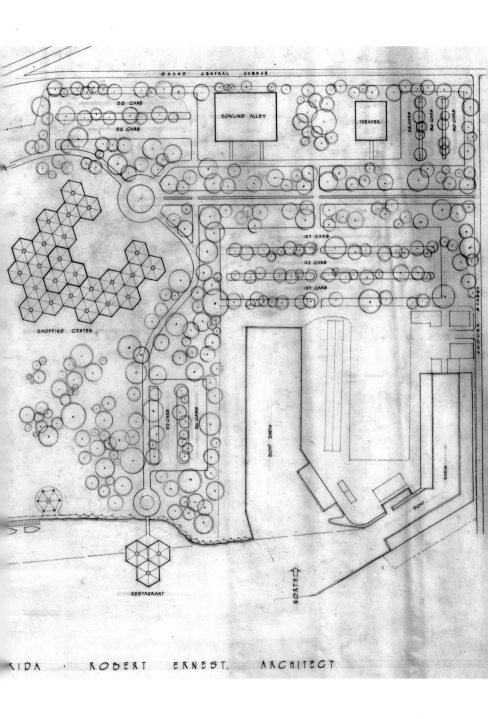

GRAND CENTRAL AVENUE

68 CARS

62 CARS

BOWLING ALLEY

THEATER

26 CARS

84 CARS

40 CARS

127 CARS

122 CARS

127 CARS

SHOPPING CENTER

BOAT BASIN

BASIN

BOAT

92 CARS

86 CARS

HOOVER STREET

NORTH

RESTAURANT

…IDA · ROBERT ERNEST, ARCHITECT

ARCHITECTURAL PRACTICE

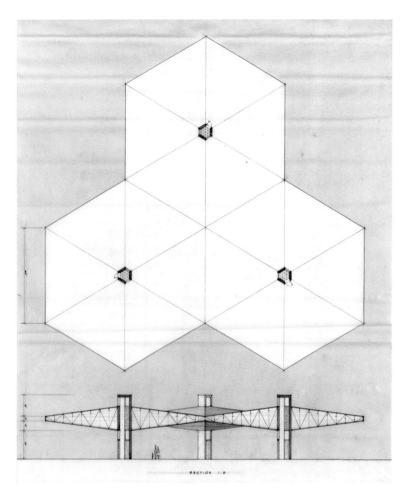

SECTION 1:6

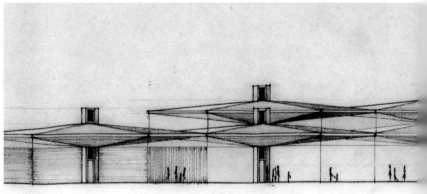

A MOMENT IN THE SUN

elegance, in its crisp geometries and cantilevered forms constructing an open and inviting shelter in the flat Florida landscape and waterscape. While the steel trusses structuring the roof canopies, which would not have been visible for the occupants, are typical in their construction, the hexagonal concrete piers that supported them, which would very much have been a part of the experience of the building, were ingenious structural inventions. Three of the pier's six sides were closed and three open, allowing the hollow interior to provide "chimney-effect" ventilation by exhausting hot air out of the top, while also introducing natural light into the interior through the structure itself.

The parallels of this remarkable design with several of Louis Kahn's contemporary projects are striking and again indicate the exceptional level of innovation Ernest's projects had achieved when he was still twenty-seven years old. Ernest's hexagonal piers that are both structural and daylight sources parallel Kahn's idea to bring natural light into his unrealized Adath Jeshurun Synagogue (1954) through the three large, hollow, triangular structural piers supporting the ceiling of the sanctuary. Even more striking—because of the fact that Ernst's 1961 design predated Kahn's—are the octagonal, sixty-foot-wide roof canopies that slope upwards from central columns at Kahn's Olivetti-Underwood Factory (1966–70).

Harry and Helene Baker House, Jacksonville, Florida (project)

The design for the Harry and Helene Baker House, which also remained unrealized due to Ernest's death, was to be located in the San José neighborhood of Jacksonville, south of downtown and on the east side of the

Fig. 3f.3 Circusland Shopping Center; plan and section of roof canopies.
Fig. 3f.4 Circusland Shopping Center; detail of entry facade.

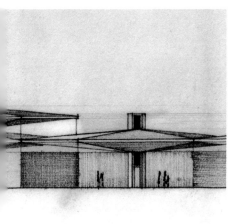

St. John's River across from the Naval Air Station. The Baker House was sited on a long lot that runs from the road to the east to the shoreline of New Rose Creek, a small tributary of the St. John's River, to the west, where the trees step down the hill and into the water. Ernest made two distinctly different designs for the Baker House. The first, dated early January 1961, organized the plan in a loose triangular configuration, with three wings containing living rooms, bedrooms, and garage and studio/guest room, respectively, which wrapped around in a pinwheel (each wing sliding past the end of the one adjacent) to form a triangular entry court. In addition, Ernest proposed a triangular-in-plan, tetrahedral-pyramid-roofed boathouse, from which a pier is extended, to be placed on the shoreline of the creek at the bottom of the hillside. There are several perspective studies of the dynamically pitched roofs of this design for the house opening large clerestory windows at the upper level and clustering around the central court, where the triangular-in-plan staircase tower anchors the composition and gives access to the roof terrace.

The plan for the second, definitive design for the Baker House is much closer to those of Ernest's other contemporary designs, such as the similar brick parallel structural walls of the Read House, as well as that of his earlier Memphis Speech and Hearing Center (fig. 3g.1). The loosely configured, U-shaped plan is centered on the large live oak tree that stands at the exact middle of the house, which is organized around a sixteen-by-forty-foot courtyard, with the entry on the west end and the east end opening towards the street. The intersection of the linear courtyard and the west, waterfront side of the U-shaped plan is anchored by a cruciform-in-plan tower that houses the dining room at the ground floor and the studio/guest room at the upper floor. The dining room opens to a large sixteen-by-sixteen-foot terrace overlooking the waterfront to the west, the floor of which is set three feet below the dining room, and to the entry foyer to the east. The studio/guest room above the dining room has large balconies cantilevering to the east over the entry and to the west towards the waterfront, with the stairs and bathroom occupying the other shorter arms of the cruciform—the whole tower a near match in miniature of the plan of the Robert Ernest House on Atlantic Beach.

The dining room and tower form the pivot point in plan where the east-west entry court to waterfront terrace axis crosses the north-south living spaces axis, with the sunken living room to the south, the dining room at the center, and the family room at the north. The wing of the Baker House along the south side of the courtyard contains at its east

Fig. 3g.1 Harry and Helene Baker House, Jacksonville, Florida (project); second, definitive design, floorplan with plan of second floor tower studio/guestroom (top left).
Fig. 3g.2 Baker House; floorplan, with corrections and dimensions marked.

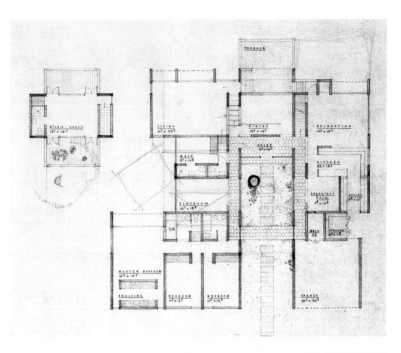

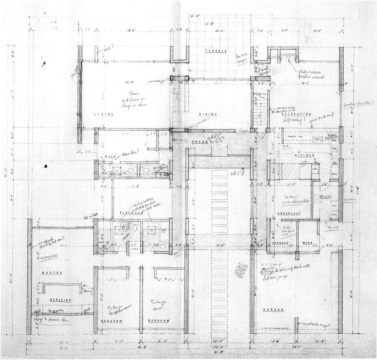

ARCHITECTURAL PRACTICE

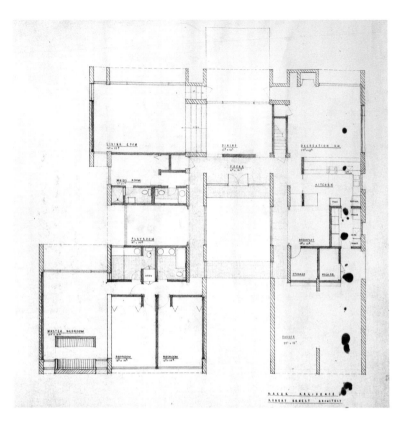

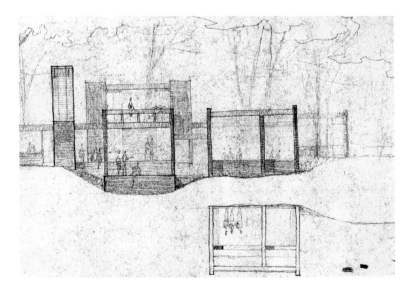

A MOMENT IN THE SUN

end the children's and parents' bedrooms, the latter set out beyond the living room to allow views of the water, with the playroom at the center, and the living room at its west end. The wing along the north side of the courtyard contains the garage at its east end, the breakfast room and kitchen at the center, and the family room at its west end. The large tree in the court stands next to the glass-walled entry porch, and the glass-walled breakfast room and adjacent kitchen on the north side open across the courtyard to the glass-walled playroom on the south side.

Though the design remained preliminary and was not developed into construction documents due to Ernest's death, the third and most resolved floorplan, of which there are two versions, indicates that the house was to be organized on a four-foot grid and structured by a series of parallel brick cavity walls running east-west, parallel to the long property lines, with two-story, U-shape-in-plan, double brick piers flanking the dining/studio block and housing the fireplace in the family room (fig.3g.2, 3g.3). The parallel brick walls largely close the house to the neighbors to the north and south and open the rooms of the house towards the road to the east and the waterfront to the west, where the windows are deeply recessed within the protective shadows of the brick piers and the roofs they carry. The wood framing of the roofs (and tower floor) of each room spans between the parallel east-west walls and, along with the varied roof heights and concrete slab-on-grade floor levels, reinforces the independent, pavilion-like character of the rooms of the house that can be seen in the sketch elevations (fig. 3g.4). The two sketch elevations indicate the different characters of the house on the flat east side of the site, where the single-story volume is opened in the center by the courtyard with its tree, and on the sloping and folding landscape of the west side, where the central dining room and lower waterfront terrace are shown nestling into the small valley descending to the creek. In its plan, massing, and elevations, the Baker House is similar to Kahn's unrealized Morris House (1955–58), which also is comprised of a loose clustering of pavilion-like rooms that were organized on a four-foot grid and structured by parallel, east-west masonry walls.

Second Baptist Church Renovation / Addition, Jacksonville Beach, Florida (project)

Ernest's unrealized design for the Second Baptist Church, led by Pastor Johnny James, proposed the addition of a new larger sanctuary on top of the existing ground-floor sanctuary, which, after completion, would

Fig. 3g.3 Baker House; floorplan.
Fig. 3g.4 Baker House; west, riverfront elevation.

be converted into the social hall. The existing church is located on the southeast corner of 3rd Avenue South, running east-west, and 8th Street South, running north-south, in Jacksonville Beach, an oceanfront community to the east of Jacksonville and north of Ponte Vedra. The existing sanctuary was a flat-roofed, one-story building with a forty-by-eighty-six-foot rectangular plan, the longer dimension running north-south, with its front entry facing north to 3rd Avenue South. Ernest's design reuses almost every element in the existing building and aligns the structural elements of the new sanctuary above with those of the existing building below (figs. 3h.1 and 3h.2). Pairs of two-story concrete block piers flank the existing brick piers and rise to the new roof above. Two lines of steel pipe columns extending from the entry to the chancel bear directly on the existing columns below. The wood framing and wood deck of the original building's roof are reused to support the new wood sanctuary floor. On the exterior, the existing brick-faced outer walls between the buttresses are extended up to meet the new concrete cap beam at the roof, and operable glass jalousie windows are opened in the new sanctuary walls on the second floor above the solid brick buttresses below. In addition, the new sanctuary is extended eight feet to the south beyond the existing building footprint to accommodate the expanded chancel, with a new storage room below.

As shown in Ernest's exterior perspective drawing, the sanctuary would have been dramatically transformed from its original horizontal proportions to its new vertical proportions—more appropriate to the religious program—largely as a result of his deployment of the series of concrete block piers that act as a new exoskeleton for the now two-story building, while also revealing the concrete block primary structure of the inner walls of both the existing building and new sanctuary. This new and more appropriate character is the result of a series of structurally necessary additions, including the seven new pairs of two-story concrete block buttresses that run along the east and west facades (figs. 3h.3 and 3h.4). Towards the southern chancel end of the sanctuary, two pairs of concrete block pier walls rise thirty-three feet from the ground to ten feet above the roof of the church, where a wooden cross is suspended, and within which are set escape stairs that descend to east and west from the area in front of the chancel. At the northern front of the church, the bell tower formed by the pair of concrete block pier walls rises thirty-six feet from the ground to twelve feet above the roof of the church, where two large wooden crosses, carrying a bell between them, are suspended, and within which is set the new glass entry doors. In front of the bell tower is set a pair of freestanding twelve-foot-tall concrete block walls, between which span the open treads of the twenty-foot-wide entry stair.

There are no perspective drawings of the interior, but the sections indicate the wood-framed, flat roof structure would be exposed, with a

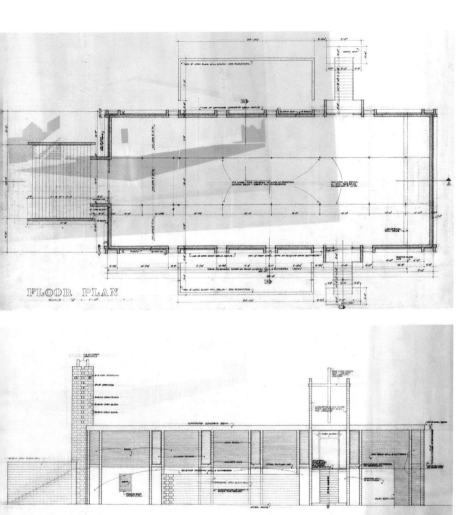

FLOOR PLAN
SCALE: ¼" = 1'-0"

RIGHT SIDE ELEVATION (LEFT SIDE ELEVATION SIMILAR, OPPOSITE HAND)
SCALE: ¼" = 1'-0"

Fig. 3h.2 Second Baptist Church; plan of new sanctuary at second floor
(stain from perspective dot-screen adhesive is on back of drawing).
Fig. 3h.3 Second Baptist Church; west elevation (east similar).

Fig. 3h.1 Second Baptist Church Renovation and Addition, Jacksonville Beach, Florida (project); perspective from street corner to northwest.

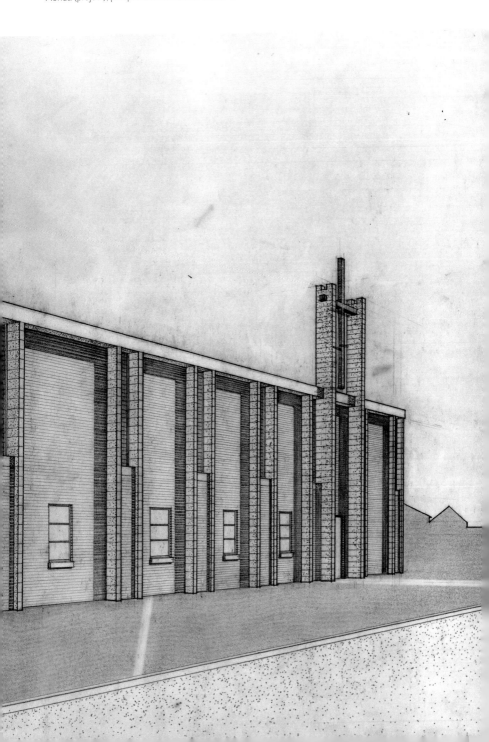

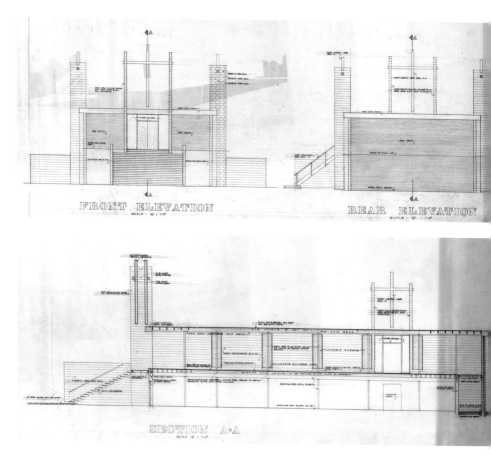

Fig. 3h.4 Second Baptist Church; north (front) and south (back) elevations.
Fig. 3h.5 Second Baptist Church; north-south longitudinal section, looking east.

pair of deep wood beams paralleling the north to south movement from the entry to the altar down the fourteen-foot-wide central nave, and closely spaced joists running east-west (fig. 3h.5). The pairs of cylindrical columns forming the central nave align with the jalousie windows set between the pairs of concrete block piers at the outer walls, and the new concrete block inner walls are exposed throughout the interior. As required by the congregation's tight budget, Ernest's design is very economical and efficient in reusing as much of the existing building as possible and in using elements necessary to strengthen the existing structure to carry the new sanctuary above, such as the vertical pairs of piers, to reinforce the vertical expression of the whole, while also exhibiting real ingenuity in the almost complete transformation of the character of the modest church building.

Other Ernest designs that remained unrealized due to his death include a shopping center in Cocoa Beach, Florida, that deployed a barrel-vaulted roof system (an elevation render of which can be seen in Ernest's studio, lower right corner of fig. 3a.14), and the commercial building renovation and new facade for the menswear shop James Helms in Jacksonville (both of late 1961) both documented in Ernest's archive. On the other hand, there are no materials or records in the Robert Ernest archives of the project for a high-rise apartment building in Jacksonville. The only documentation of this project is in the article, "In Memoriam: Robert Ernest," authored by the photographer Robert Pottinger, a friend of Ernest's from their time together in architecture school at the University of Virginia, which was published in the 1965 double issue of the Yale architectural journal, *Perspecta 9/10*, dedicated to Ernest's memory.[35]

In the article, Pottinger indicates that the apartment tower was one of "several urban redevelopment projects for the city of Jacksonville" that Ernest worked on in 1961, another being the Youth Center, the last building examined in this chapter. The Jacksonville high-rise apartment project is documented only in two model photographs in *Perspecta 9/10*, showing a plan view of the roof and a view from the side (figs. 3i.1 and 3i.2). Intriguingly, unlike the other materials published in *Perspecta 9/10*, all of which come from Ernest's archives, the photographs of the apartment tower were taken by A. Robert Faesy, an undergraduate student in the architecture program at Yale from 1959 to 1963, who, during the summers, was responsible for documenting student work for the school archives and for use in *Perspecta*.[36] The fact that these photographs were taken by Faesy while he was at Yale suggests that most likely the model for the apartment tower was brought to Yale by Pottinger as part of the *In Memoriam: Robert Ernest* exhibit that Pottinger organized in the architecture school sometime before the publication of *Perspecta 9/10*.[37]

Ernest's design for the apartment tower in Jacksonville is a highly resolved deployment of the hexagonal and triangular plan geometries to be found in other projects, including the Eli Becker House and the Circusland Shopping Center, and the stacking of apartments is similar to that in his New Haven housing towers project designed while he was at Yale. It is intriguing to note that in one of Ernest's sketches for the New Haven housing project, he drew palm trees on the apartment terraces, suggesting he revisited and likely drew from the Yale project sketches in this later Jacksonville housing project. In fact, due to its use of hexagonal rather than rectilinear geometry, the Jacksonville apartment tower design combines the two different apartment cluster options Ernest explored in the Yale project—stair towers at the corners and stair towers at the center of each side. But the sectional complexity of the Jacksonville apartment tower, with single- and double-height volumes interlocking around the perimeter of the building, is a significant advance on his earlier work.

The overall plan of the nine-story tower is a hexagon, with a larger solid-walled hexagonal structural, mechanical and stair core at the center, and six smaller, solid-walled hexagonal structural and service cores set along the outer edge of each of the floorplan's six straight sides, with the floors spanning from the central core to the peripheral core columns, and from one peripheral core column to the next. (This use of the larger and smaller hexagonal service towers is shared with the Eli Becker House plan). Each floor slab is opened with three hexagonal voids between the central and peripheral cores, forming double-height interior rooms or covered terraces that bring daylight deep into the plan. The locations of the double-height voids in plan alternate on every other floor, so that each single-height room has a double-height room adjacent, sometimes on the same floor and sometimes on the floor below. Again, the parallels to the contemporary work of Louis Kahn can be felt in this remarkable project, which may be said to exemplify Kahn's belief that, unlike ancient architects who built with solid columns, contemporary architects build with "hollow columns," within which the services are housed, so that the servant spaces frame and form the spaces they serve.

Fig. 3i.1 Apartment Tower, Jacksonville (project); view of model from above.
Fig. 3i.2 Apartment Tower; view of model from side.

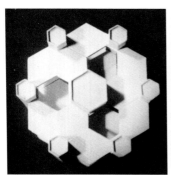

Municipal Youth Center, Jacksonville, Florida, 1961-62

Ernest's last realized design, constructed after his death (and thus without his supervision), was the Municipal Youth Center (now named the Joseph Lee Center), located to the west of Evergreen Cemetery in north Jacksonville, on a 130-by-255-foot city-owned site running between Perry Street to the east, onto which the building fronted, and Springfield Street to the west (fig. 3j.1). On the north side, one half of the right of way of 42nd Street was closed by city ordinance to make space for the new building. Ernest began work on what was first named a "recreation center" on August 30, 1960, less than three months after establishing his practice in Jacksonville, when he sketched the basic three-bay scheme for the building at the bottom of a set of meeting notes documenting the preliminary program for the approximately 5,000-square-foot building with an estimated budget of $75,000. However, it was not until more than fifteen months later, after the design was already completed, that the formal contract with the City of Jacksonville for the Youth Center commission, to be undertaken by the engineers George R. Register and Morris V. Cummings (consultants of Ernest on several other projects) and Ernest, doing business as "Register & Cummings and Robert Ernest, Associated Architect and Engineers," was drawn up and dated December 5, 1961, and the contract was not ratified by the Jacksonville City Council until January 17, 1962.

Starting in the fall of 1960, Ernest developed the design with two different roof configurations, but the floorplan was established from the beginning (figs. 3j.2 and 3j.3). The single-story rectangular cruciform plan was composed of three primary, twenty-by-forty-foot bays running east-west, over which were placed vaulted concrete roof shells. The primary bays were separated and framed at their ends by ten-by-forty-foot bays, with pairs of ten-foot-deep concrete fin walls carrying concrete beams spanning across the main central room and supporting the outer edges of the roof vaults. The alternating ten-by-twenty-foot and ten-by-ten-foot spaces along the eastern and western sides of the central vaulted room housed the support functions and services. These included the recessed covered main entrance located in the central twenty-foot-wide bay on the east side, and the two recessed, covered exits (also giving access from the proposed parking) located in the two ten-foot-wide bays to either side of the central bay on the west side. In Ernest's first design, of which a model was built, the three large twenty-by-forty-foot roof vaults are thin curving barrel vaults, which, while to be built in concrete and carried on precast concrete beams with integral rainwater gutters, are strikingly similar to the curved plywood barrel vaults of the Jacksonville studio/residence Ernest designed for James Roy in 1958.

The final design of the Youth Center comprises a forty-by-one-hundred-foot central room, covered by three, half-hexagonal-in-section

folded plate, cast-in-place reinforced concrete vaults, twenty feet wide and spanning forty feet, a double square proportion (figs. 3j.4, 3j.5, and 3j.6). Though the room was constructed as a forty-by-one-hundred-foot space, the floorplans, including the final construction drawings, all show an alternate where the exterior walls of the two ten-by-forty-foot spaces at the north and south ends of the main room are recessed ten feet and

Fig. 3j.1 Municipal Youth Center, Jacksonville, Florida, 1961–62; final design, presentation perspective, aerial view from northeast.

Fig. 3j.2 Municipal Youth Center; site plan for final design.
Fig. 3j.3 Municipal Youth Center; first design, floorplan, and curved roof vaults.

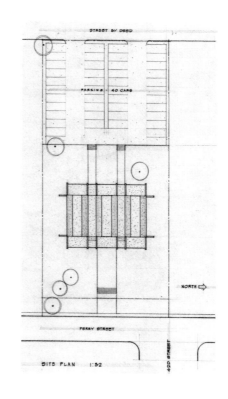

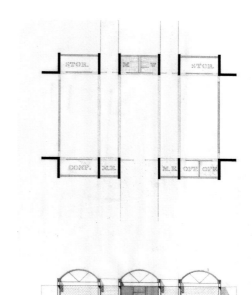

ARCHITECTURAL PRACTICE

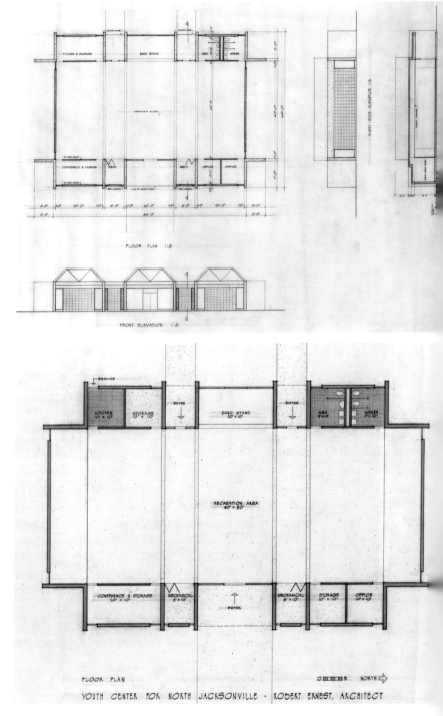

YOUTH CENTER FOR NORTH JACKSONVILLE · ROBERT ERNEST, ARCHITECT

A MOMENT IN THE SUN

placed at the edge of the roof vault, forming a forty-by-eighty-foot room (a double square matching the dimensions of the galleries of Kahn's Yale Art Gallery, site of Ernest's studio classes). The outer edges of the roof vaults bear on pairs of two-foot, eight-inch deep, one-foot-wide, cast-in-place, reinforced concrete beams that run between the pairs of one-foot-wide, eleven-foot-deep, cast-in-place, reinforced concrete fin walls on the east and west sides of the building (figs. 3j.7 and 3j.8). The north and south ends of the roof vault sequence are braced by one-foot-wide, eleven-foot-deep, cast-in-place, reinforced concrete fin walls that form four solid reentrant corners for the main central room, and which give the plan its cruciform shape. The non-load-bearing infill walls between the cast-in-place concrete fin walls on all four exterior sides of the building are made of eight-inch concrete blocks set in a stack bond, and the non-load-bearing interior infill walls along the west and east sides of the main room are made of four-inch concrete blocks set in a stack bond (fig. 3j.9). The four-inch concrete floor slab is elevated eight-inches above the exterior grade and is topped by one-inch white-colored terrazzo, producing the finished interior floor. The lines of the pairs of concrete beams carrying the roof vaults are inscribed into the terrazzo floor by brass divider strips. Brass terrazzo divider strips divide the forty-foot span of the room down its center, forming twenty-by-twenty-foot squares, and they run along the east and west edges of the main room at the walls and thresholds of the secondary spaces (fig. 3j.14).

The main space can be used as a single room for dancing (the original program indicated "60 to 100 couples") and other large events employing the concrete curb-edged and plywood-floored stage or "band stand," elevated eight inches above the main floor, which is located in the ten-by-twenty-foot, glass-walled space on the west side, opposite the entry. Ernest planned for the main space to be subdivisible into three spaces defined by the roof vaults if needed, though there is no evidence that this was ever implemented. The ten-by-forty-foot spaces at the southern and northern ends of the main room have shuffleboard court patterns set into the terrazzo flooring. The four ten-by-twenty-foot spaces (double squares) to the east and west of the main room contain a conference room, office, storage, bathrooms, and kitchen, which has a central pass-through window to the main room and a service doorway from the western, rear side of the building. The two ten-by-ten-foot spaces (single squares) to either side of the entry, accessed by full-width wood louver double doors, contain the mechanical equipment that feeds directly into the two mechanical chases located above the ceilings that are hung between the pairs of concrete beams supporting the roof vaults.

Fig. 3j.4 Municipal Youth Center; preliminary design, plan, elevations, and transverse section.
Fig. 3j.5 Municipal Youth Center; final floorplan.

ARCHITECTURAL PRACTICE

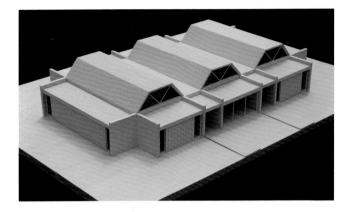

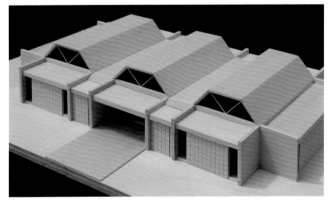

Fig. 3j.7 Municipal Youth Center; aerial perspective view of model from southeast (model made under author's supervision).
Fig. 3j.8 Municipal Youth Center; aerial perspective view of model from northeast.
Fig. 3j.9 Municipal Youth Center; view of east, entry facade of model.

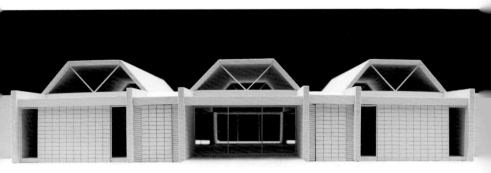

A MOMENT IN THE SUN

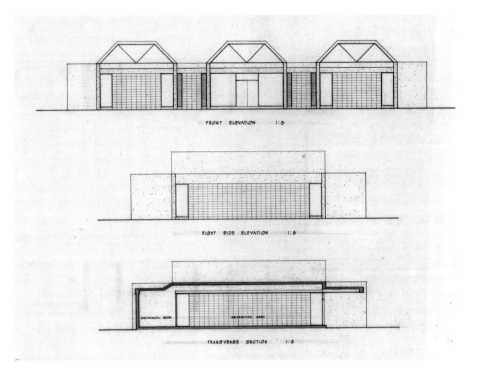

FRONT ELEVATION 1:8

RIGHT SIDE ELEVATION 1:8

MECHANICAL ROOM   RECREATION AREA

TRANSVERSE SECTION 1:8

Fig. 3j.6 Municipal Youth Center; final front and side elevations, transverse section.
Fig. 3j.11 Municipal Youth Center; view of entry vault of model.

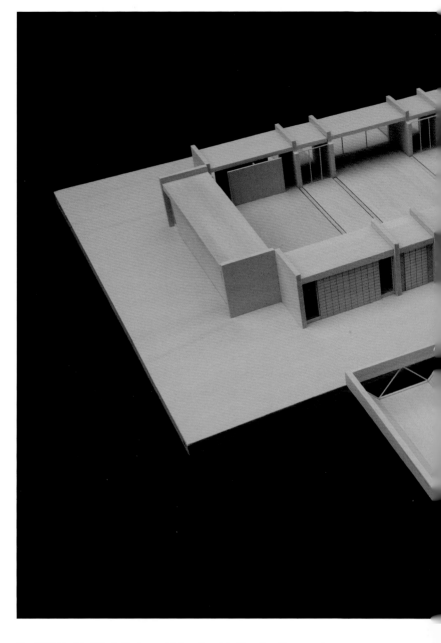

Fig. 3j.10 Municipal Youth Center; aerial view of model with roof vaults removed (model made under author's supervision).

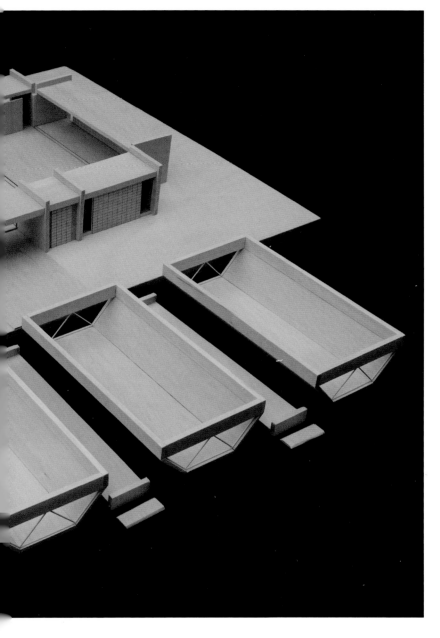

ARCHITECTURAL PRACTICE

The ceiling heights inside vary from sixteen feet, four inches at the top of the vaults, to eight feet, eight inches at the bottom of the concrete beams at the lower edges of the vaults, to nine feet, eight inches in the ten-foot-deep spaces on all four sides of the building (fig. 3j.10). The large, open east and west ends of the concrete folded plate roof vaults are glazed in triangular sections and provide the majority of the daylight to the central room. Daylight also enters through the glass-walled entry and elevated bandstand, set across from each other at the center of the building, as well as the vertical, three-foot, five-inch-wide, floor-to-ceiling windows set against the structural concrete walls in the corners of the other four twenty-foot-wide support spaces to the east and west, where they align with the doors opening off the central room, and in the corners of the forty-foot-wide spaces at the north and south ends of the main room (figs. 3j.11, 3j.12, and 3j.13). These vertical windows, set in the corner of the rooms, illuminate the concrete structural walls, and they demarcate a line of light between the structural concrete and nonstructural concrete block infill walls—a detail that can be found in the work of both Wright and Kahn. Floor-to-ceiling, one-foot, four-inch-wide aluminum ventilation louvers separate the structural concrete fin walls from the nonstructural concrete block infill walls at the exteriors of the two mechanical rooms (figs. 3j.14 and 3j.15).

Six sets of linear, fluorescent tube electrical uplights, two for each roof vault, are integrated in square, plastered coves running along the inner edges of the bottoms of the concrete beams, their light bouncing off the roof vaults to indirectly illuminate the room. The reinforced concrete roof vaults were cast in reusable formwork, with neoprene roofing applied on the exterior. On the interior, half-inch thick white acoustic plaster cladding was applied to the folded and flat portions of the concrete roof vaults, the concrete beams, and the two mechanical duct chases between the three vaults. The white aggregate cast concrete walls were complemented by the buff-colored limestone aggregate of the locally manufactured concrete masonry block walls. The terrazzo floor and the concrete block and cast concrete walls, none of which require painting, were intended to respond to the charge of designing a building that would be "maintenance free." The construction drawings for the Youth Center were drafted by the Register and Cummings office and initialed as "checked" by Ernest and are dated April 10, 1962.

The Youth Center's semi-hexagonal-in-section folded plate reinforced concrete roof shells were among the earliest generation of such structures to be constructed in the United States, and Ernest's structure predates by ten years Louis Kahn's first realization of a similar structure at the Kimbell Museum of 1972. The entire fabric of the Youth Center exemplifies Kahn's ideas of servant and served spaces, exposing the structure and materials of construction, and the structure as the "giver of light"—concepts that Kahn had first articulated only in the late 1950s during the period he was designing the similar long-span folded-plate precast

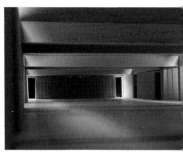

Fig. 3j.12 Municipal Youth Center; interior view of central roof vault of model looking west (model made under author's supervision).
Fig. 3j.13 Municipal Youth Center; interior view of main room, looking south.

concrete structures for the Trenton Jewish Community Center of 1958 and the first scheme for the laboratories of the Salk Institute of 1960–62. The fact that Kahn's Salk Institute was in development at the exact same time as Ernest's Youth Center again indicates Ernest's remarkable level of achievement at age twenty-eight (fig. 3j.16).

Ernest had finalized the design for the Youth Center well before the contract with the City was drawn up on November 29, 1961, and signed on January 17, 1962. In an undated draft layout and notes likely intended for a press release, Ernest included a sketch of the aerial perspective (which shows pairs of circular skylights, similar to those in his Yale high school project, above the support spaces on the east and west sides of the main room), surrounded by his description of the building and its varied uses. In the main room, he notes that table games can be "quickly stored to provide a large hall for dancing," the hall can be "divided into three smaller units described by the vaults," and the electric lighting is to be set "in integral coves along beam sides." He also provides a brief description of the materials of white "poured-in-place reinforced concrete," buff-colored "lime concrete masonry block," and spray-applied white acoustic plaster on the roof vaults, as well as the methods of construction, including the idea of employing moveable, reusable formwork to cast the concrete roof vaults.

When the project was announced in early 1962 in the *Jacksonville Journal*, the article carried Ernest's beautifully rendered aerial perspective of the final design but did not mention any of his talking points from his draft press release (fig. 3j.1). The article noted the city council's hope that "with the successful operation of this facility and its endorsement by the community, this will be the start of a citywide program of youth centers." The center was to be operated by the city recreation department and would have a full-time youth director. To be built of "maintenance-free," integrally colored materials, "making paint unnecessary," the article noted that the modest building would cost $59,000 (for 5,600 square feet), or around $10.54 per square foot. While noting that it was "possible to build the facility for a cheaper price," the city believed that they needed a building that would be "attractive, to appeal to the teenagers."[38] The article indicated that construction of the Youth Center was estimated to start in mid-May and would be ready for operation in mid-September.

Robert Ernest did not live to see the Youth Center—his only realized public building as well as arguably his greatest work—constructed, completed, and opened for use. Beginning in late 1961, Ernest became increasingly ill with rapidly spreading melanoma cancer and eventually was unable to continue working on a number of projects, including some that were quite far along in their development, none of which would be realized. Yet Ernest continued to receive visitors to his office at 360 Beach Avenue, and he continued to check and approve the construction drawings for the Youth Center, having blueprints made of the revised construction drawings being drafted by the Register and Cummings office as late as April 4, 1962. On May 10, 1962, days before the Youth Center would start construction, and only six months after the birth of his second daughter, Kristen, Robert Ernest passed away at the age of twenty-eight.

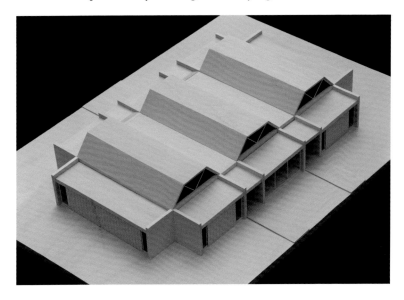

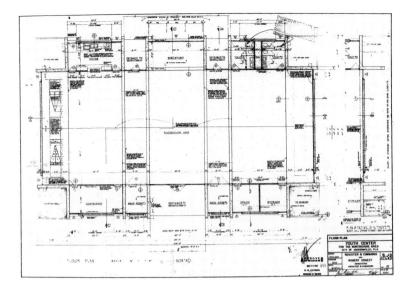

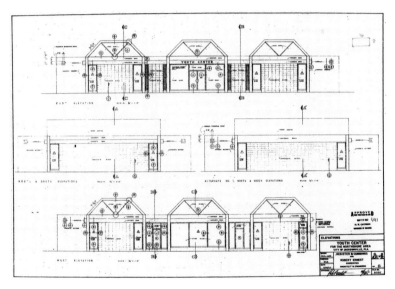

Fig. 3j.16 Municipal Youth Center; aerial view of model from southeast (model made under author's supervision).

Fig. 3j.14 Municipal Youth Center; floorplan, construction drawings.
Fig. 3j.15 Municipal Youth Center; elevations, construction drawings.

ARCHITECTURAL PRACTICE

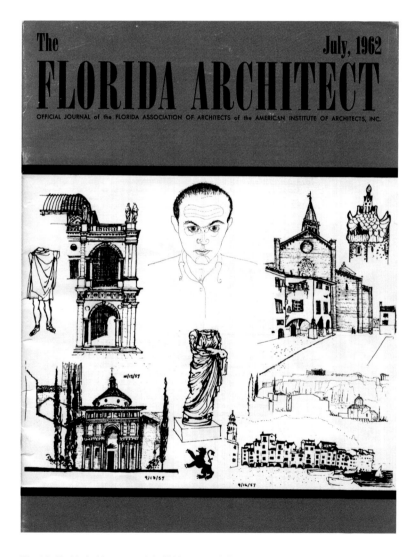

Fig. 4.1 *Florida Architect* cover, July 1962 issue, with Ernest travel sketches and self-portrait.

Legacy and Influence

The month Robert Ernest passed away, his home and studio in Atlantic Beach was selected as a "Record House" and published in the May 1962 issue of *Architectural Record*, the most prestigious award given for single-family houses in the United States. As I have noted, three of Ernest's designs—the Memphis Airport, the Memphis Speech and Hearing Center, and the Ernest House—earlier received *Progressive Architecture* Awards for designs not yet built in the January 1961 issue of *Progressive Architecture*. Immediately after his death, Ernest's life and career were celebrated by the Jacksonville AIA with an exhibit at the Jacksonville Art Museum on June 3, 1962, and by the publication of his work and dedication of the July 1962 issue of the *Florida Architect* to Ernest's memory, with his travel sketches and self-portrait on the cover (fig. 4.1). Three years later, Ernest's work was celebrated with an exhibition at Yale University and published in the 1965 issue of *Perspecta 9 /10*, which was dedicated to his memory. Following these remembrances, Ernest and his work were almost entirely lost to memory for nearly sixty years, the only exceptions being the inclusion of the Ernest House in the 1974 book *Houses Architects Design for Themselves*, which reproduces the 1962 *Architectural Record* "Record Houses" article and the entry in the late Jan Hochstim's *Florida Modern*, published in 2004, a catalog of the work of Florida modern architects during the years 1945 to 1970, which presents the Becker and Ernest Houses.[39] Ernest's three realized works, as well as his remarkable unrealized projects, may be said to have disappeared from disciplinary history.

The three buildings constructed to Ernest's designs have had varied afterlives. After his passing, Ernest's widow, Lynwood, and their daughters, Kim and Kristen, lived in the Ernest House in Atlantic Beach, where the girls spent their youth. In 1993, with the girls grown, Lynwood moved to a smaller apartment, after which the new owners of the Ernest House made an addition to the west side, matching the original house in mass and detail but modifying the section and blocking the studio's access to the exterior. At some point the entire exterior of the house was painted, covering the previously exposed block. In a stroke of good fortune, in 1995–96, the Becker House was beautifully renovated for its new owners by Jacksonville architect William Morgan, a lifelong admirer of Ernest's work, and today the house appears almost exactly as it did when it was first constructed.

Sadly, Ernest's last building and his only public work, the north Jacksonville Municipal Youth Center, was never built according to his original design, and due to later renovations can no longer be experienced even in its original, adulterated condition. During the period of Ernest's illness with cancer in the spring of 1962, the engineers of record, Register and Cummings, modified the final construction drawings of April 10, 1962, to eliminate the beams at the bottom edges of the roof vaults (leaving only those at the north and south ends of the vaults), so that only the six-inch concrete slab spans across the two ten-by-forty-foot spaces between the three vaults. While the edge beams are not well documented in Ernest's drawings of the Youth Center that still exist, which include no longitudinal sections, he references "reinforced cast-in-place concrete beams," both early and late in the design process, in the early sketches and in his text for the spring 1962 press release intended to be given to the Jacksonville newspapers. It is not clear whether Ernest agreed to this change, though it is recorded on the architectural drawings of the construction set, which carries Ernest's initials, indicating that they were "checked" and presumably approved by him (though all the initials on the drawings appear to be in the same hand, suggesting a single author at Register and Cummings). In any event, the result is that the folded-plate roof structure is no longer visible from below, as it is hidden beneath the nonstructural plastered duct chase space that was suspended in the position originally to be occupied by the vault edge beams. Whatever the timing, this constitutes a fundamental change in Ernest's original structural conception of the vaults, each of which was intended to be structurally integrated with its pair of edge beams.

In a second change, which was even less likely to have received Ernest's approval, the Register and Cummings engineers also modified the structural drawings so that all the ten-foot-deep structural fin walls that Ernest had designed to be cast-in-place concrete, and which are shown as being concrete in the floorplans of the April 10, 1962, construction drawings, were changed to concrete masonry blocks set in a structural running bond, which were then coated with stucco inside and outside to conceal their joint pattern and make them look like cast-concrete. Over the years the concrete block walls (which are not as strong as cast-concrete walls) have shifted beneath the roof loads, producing extensive diagonal cracks, and the applied stucco has decayed to reveal the concrete block pattern beneath; the resulting contrast of the non-load-bearing stack bond of the infill walls and the load-bearing running bond of the structural fin walls marred the clarity of Ernest's simple but powerful design.

Fig. 4.2 View of the framing for the new, second roof above original roof of Municipal Youth Center, with original concrete vault beneath, June 1997; photograph by William Morgan.

Then, thirty-five years later, in June 1997, Ernest's client, the City of Jacksonville, vandalized their own building by constructing a wood-framed, pitched metal roof covering the entire original concrete folded-plate roof, with pediments at the north and south ends and over the entry (fig. 4.2). The possible reasons for this vandalism might include the difficulty of maintaining the original neoprene roofing, yet in fact the low-slope roofing products available to repair the roof in the 1990s were far more durable and flexible than those from the 1960s. Another more compelling reason might be that the uninsulated concrete roof vaults allowed too much heat to penetrate the interior. But rather than put a new roof over the entire building and covering the clerestory windows, it would have been more appropriate to add insulation and a new metal roof following the contours of the concrete vaults (similar to the way Kahn's Kimbell Museum's curving vaults are roofed and insulated), thus preserving the hexagonal folding forms of the roof structure by thickening their profiles, and maintaining the daylight from the clerestory windows. Today the original concrete folded-plate ceiling remains visible inside the main room, but the six large clerestory windows at the ends, their glazing still intact, are covered by the new roof, darkening the interior and necessitating the use of electric lighting at all times of the day.[40] However, the original concrete roof vaults remain beneath the new roof, which can be removed as easily as it was installed, and one hopes that someday civic leaders of the City of Jacksonville will see the wisdom of returning the building to its original condition, with appropriate updates.

Despite his almost complete disappearance from the disciplinary history of architecture today, it can be argued that Robert Ernest was a key player in the evolution of modern architecture in Florida after 1960. Even though he only realized three built works, Ernst had considerable influence on his contemporaries in Florida as well as on following generations of Florida architects. This has taken the form of direct influence through Ernest's three built works—his only designs that were known—as well as a more indirect influence with respect to transmitting principles of design and construction often identified with Louis Kahn, and in particular, the expressive and exposed use of building materials such as concrete block.

A group of Florida architects working after 1960 can be said to be part of what I have called a "concrete block school," inspired by Ernest's three built works, all of which employed concrete blocks, as well as the earlier concrete block works of Frank Lloyd Wright and Paul Rudolph. The architects that may be considered part of this group were scattered throughout the state of Florida, and so were only partly the result of Ernest's local influence. In Ernest's own work as well as that of this group, it was the proximity of the manufacturers of concrete block that played a key part in the emergence of the "concrete block school." From the 1940s to 1970s, locally manufactured concrete blocks were available everywhere in Florida, with one or more manufacturing plants a few miles from almost any building site. Very low-tech by today's building material standards, concrete blocks were made with local sand and limestone aggregates, and as a result varied in color (with names such as Ocala block, gray-tan in color, and St. Augustine block, yellow-tan in color), and blocks were custom cast for every job, and thus did not need to be standardized sizes or shapes. As every manufacturing job was custom, concrete blocks were often cast in architect-designed metal forms at no extra cost, allowing each building to have unique pattern imprints similar to those Wright put on the blocks used in his buildings at Florida Southern College, or of unique shape, as in the case of the rhomboid-shaped blocks Ernest used to build the Eli Becker House.

The works of William Morgan constitute some of the most important contributions to the "concrete block school." Morgan, who apparently just missed meeting Ernest in the late summer of 1955 when they came within days of overlapping in Rudolph's Cambridge office,[41] became aware of Ernest's work when, after graduating from Harvard—where he did his undergraduate studies with Walter Gropius, followed by a tour of duty in the Navy, and then graduate studies with José Luis Sert—he returned to Jacksonville to establish his own practice in 1964. During his distinguished career, Morgan developed three modes of working in the Florida landscape: the "earth" projects, involving buried, excavated, and bermed constructions; the "tree" projects, involving structures cantilevered from central piers; and the "tower" projects, involving constructions elevated and unfolding above the landscape.[42] In Morgan's tower projects, Ernest's house in Atlantic Beach was a critical inspiration, as exemplified in one of Morgan's late works, the Dylan Morgan House (2003) for his son's family in Atlantic Beach, where, like Ernest, he employed a variation on the interlocking section of Le Corbusier's Carthage Villa project. Morgan, who, as mentioned above, was commissioned to renovate and restore Ernest's Becker House in 1995–96, employed concrete block, including the "ribbed" bush-hammered block favored by Rudolph, in almost all of his hundreds of built works.

Among other architects who were Ernest's contemporaries, and thus can be considered his fellow travelers in the development of a type of modern architecture appropriate to Florida, is Robert Broward, who after working as an apprentice at Frank Lloyd Wright's Taliesin, returned to Jacksonville to design a series of Wright-inspired works, such as the Unitarian Church (1965), with its soaring wood-framed ceiling and roof set on parallel concrete block sidewalls, as well as prototype housing projects such as the Laurel Grove (1957) housing subdivision, a series of modest but spatially rich dwellings constructed with standard concrete blocks. Broward, who authored the moving essay in remembrance of Ernest published in the July 1962 issue of *Florida Architect*, was quick to acknowledge the inspiration he had drawn from Ernest's works. Also worth noting is the Hollywood, Florida, architect Charles Reed Jr., who employed stack-bonded concrete blocks in almost all his built works, and whose two-story, tower-like Wicker House (1959) employs a cruciform plan that is remarkably similar to that of the Robert Ernest House of the next year. Despite having a distinguished career with numerous built works, Reed, like Ernest, is largely absent from the histories of Florida modern architecture.

Among the architects who were near contemporaries of Ernest and in whose work the influence of Ernest's buildings may be discerned is Winter Park architect Lowell Lotspeich, whose Cassel Residence (1964) is a complex spatial composition employing concrete blocks to form a series of independent and interconnected volumes. Also in this group is Dan Duckham, whose Reed Residence (1964) in Fort Lauderdale is a masterful hexagonal grid–planned composition of custom-formed, stack-bonded concrete blocks. While relationship of this design to Wright's Hanna House (1936) in Palo Alto is unmistakable, so too is the possible influence of Ernest's Becker House. Tampa architect Dwight Holmes's residence (1969) is rectangular in plan, with four solid concrete block sidewalls framing the three-story volume, which is opened at the center, and both ends. As in Ernest's house, the section is a variation on Le Corbusier's Carthage Villa project, with double-height spaces alternating at the east and west ends of the plan. Miami architect Milton Harry's Nyitray Residence (1968–70) is a collection of rectangular room volumes constructed entirely of massive concrete block walls that define the rooms and pass through the glass to join outside and inside.

The works of the architect considered to be the youngest member of the original Sarasota School, Carl Abbott, who has practiced his entire career in Sarasota, indicate the subtle yet continuing influence of Ernest's work on Florida architects. Abbott was exposed to Ernest's work early, when after graduating from the University of Florida and working in the offices of Mark Hampton and Bert Brosmith (a former associate of Paul Rudolph), he was accepted into the Master of Architecture degree program at Yale University. Before heading north in late summer of 1961, Abbott came to Jacksonville to meet Robert Ernest at his own home and studio at Atlantic Beach, to discuss Ernest's experiences with Rudolph at Yale, and to visit Rudolph's Milam House, the construction of which Ernest had supervised. While Abbott often prefers to clad the concrete block structural walls of his buildings in stucco plaster, in a number of Sarasota projects such as the Deering Bayfront Residence (1975), the Artist's Family Compound (2001), and his own studio (2023), the influence of Ernest's flush joint detailing of the running bond concrete block walls—as opposed to the recessed joints of the stack bond concrete block walls of the Sarasota School—may be discerned even today.

The works of Fort Lauderdale architect Donald Singer are at once the preeminent examples of the "concrete block school," and evidence of Ernest's influence on Florida architecture from the 1960s to today. Singer visited Wright's Florida Southern buildings while an undergraduate at the University of Florida, and, after completing his graduate studies at Columbia University in 1961, during which time he met Louis Kahn, Singer returned to Florida to establish his practice, at which point he became aware of Ernest's three built works. Singer's earliest work, the Academy Animal Hospital (1964), is a composition of interlocking rectangular volumes that deploys concrete block as the primary construction material. In the Weinberger Residence (1968), three rectangular concrete block–walled volumes are rotated to form a pinwheel plan, and the apertures employ daylight to articulate the joints between the concrete block volumes. In Singer's Medical Office Building (1972), three solid, concrete block–walled masses, integrally cast with concrete floor and roof beams, span across the large street-level openings leading to the covered and shaded parking beneath the buildings at grade, and the medical offices, cantilevered at each end, are raised to the second level, where they open to central linear courts.

A coda of sorts to Singer's engagement of Ernest's legacy in Florida came in 1967, when Singer, Lowell Lotspeich, and Milton Harry were appointed as the publications committee for the Florida Association of the AIA. While serving as the editor of the *Florida Architect*, Singer was asked to propose a cover photograph for a special publication on residential architecture, tentatively titled "Florida Architecture." Singer approached Jerry Uelsmann, the University of Florida professor and renowned photographer and creator of darkroom mergers of multiple black-and-white images through a process he called "post-visualization" and asked if he would photograph the Robert Ernest House and create a cover image with it. The resulting photographic print is of the western facade of the Robert Ernest House, which appears to float over the reflection, not of itself, but of an inverted Florida Cracker house (fig. 4.3). Uelsmann's juxtaposition of modern and vernacular Florida houses deftly suggests the very real parallels between the ways both houses employ what we today call sustainable—passive and energy-saving ways of engaging the natural environment—and suggests that, despite their formal differences, the two houses provide very similar experiences of the Florida landscape for their occupants. When the AIA Board declined to use it, Singer used the photograph as the cover of the September 1967 issue of the *Florida Architect*.[43]

In conclusion, the materials presented in this book make it clear that Robert Ernest was a remarkably talented and unusually gifted architectural designer, whose future promise and potential was inestimable. Ernest's two built works, both realized before he had turned twenty-eight, and one work built after his death, as well as the remarkably innovative unrealized projects documented in his archives, clearly indicate that if Ernest had lived to a normal lifespan, he would have without question been one of the most important architects of his generation, with the potential to design precedent-setting buildings equal to those realized by the most recognized architects in the sixty years after his death.

A MOMENT IN THE SUN

Afterwords

Robert Broward

In Memoriam: Robert Griffith Ernest, 1933–1962
On May 10, 1962, a tragic death occurred in Jacksonville. Robert Griffith Ernest, only twenty-eight and destined to be one of the greatest architects of America, fell victim to melanoma, a vicious, fast-growing form of cancer. He was a graduate of Yale University and had worked extensively with Paul Rudolph. The following statement is by [Robert Broward for] *the Jacksonville chapter of the AIA, of which* [Ernest] *was a member.*

In a society where the apathetic acceptance of ugliness through default has become a tragic reality, sometimes a bright and shining star of hope appears on the scene, cutting through the fragmented confusion to reveal, in a very special way, sensible order and sensitive beauty. Robert Ernest was such an illumination for all who knew him.

There are many men who are known as architects in our society, but a handful are architects in the highest sense; and of this handful, Bob was destined to be one of the true leaders. He was totally involved in the art of architecture and through his rare combination of creative ability and conscious responsibility, everything he designed was a potential work of art—in danger of not being so only because of other forces at work in our society over which the artist has little control.

His completed works are few . . . he had been on his own for but two years. But in those two years he produced works far surpassing the best of most architects who have been in practice for many years. Each project held within it the wonderment of creation for this man, a new chance to say something beautiful about a world that has forgotten what a wondrous thing beauty is. For this alone Bob has left an indelible imprint upon the practice of those who care about beauty in a vending machine culture.

The handful of buildings completed from his studio are statements which have been accorded the acclaim of the best architectural critics in America. We are fortunate that these buildings are in our community. We are fortunate that Bob Ernest lived here the tragically short time allotted

Fig. 4.3 Jerry Uelsmann photographic collage of Robert Ernest House and vernacular Florida Cracker house.

to him. The buildings speak for themselves and for Bob as any fine work of art must . . . and to see them is better than to read of them. On June 3, [1962,] in the Jacksonville Art Museum, a special exhibit of the work of Bob Ernest was held so that what he believed and what he was trying to do may be better seen and understood by all of us.

A truly great artist has lived here and though he is now gone, the principles he understood so well remain as always. And as we grope for a fuller meaning in our own lives through them, Bob Ernest will be remembered.

—July 1962, Florida Architect

Carl Abbott

On a late summer day in 1961, Robert Ernest was showing me around Rudolph's nearly completed Milam House.

I was in Atlantic Beach to see the much-anticipated Milam House, to see Robert Ernest's architecture (which I had read about), and to talk with Robert about his earlier experience in Rudolph's Master Class at Yale.

My drive was from Sarasota to Jacksonville to Yale, where I was to be one of fifteen graduate students in Rudolph's upcoming Master Class. After getting my degree in 1959 from the University of Florida, I had been working in Sarasota for Bert Brosmith, who had been one of the lead architects in Rudolph's famous Sarasota office. On one of Rudolph's infrequent Sarasota visits, I met him and asked about the Milam House; Rudolph said get in touch with Robert Ernest, a very talented architect who was carrying out the construction administration on Milam.

Robert Ernest was very generous with his time. I remember meeting him at his office in a boat dock house on the St. John's River in downtown Jacksonville, where he led me through his projects on the drawing boards, and we talked about Yale. We then drove to Rudolph's Milam House at Ponte Vedra for a thorough walk-through.

Afterwards we went to Robert's own home and studio in Atlantic Beach, which was under construction. I recall the interplay of the vertical volumes that were just taking form. Also, the large exposed concrete block walls and the manner in which the blocks were installed running bond with flush joints, which gave the wall a monolithic strength. This is in contrast to the more refined block detailing of the Sarasota School stacked bond with clearly recessed joints. Later while at Yale, on a trip to see Louis Kahn's Trenton Bath House, I saw this same monolithic detailing on the exposed concrete block walls. Here in my Sarasota office I have used this same monolithic detailing on a number of projects. Currently I am using this detailing in the construction of the large exposed concrete block walls of my own Studio.

That same afternoon, we returned to Robert's office in the boat dock house where we continued our discussion of Paul Rudolph at Yale. Robert talked about how demanding Rudolph could be—challenging you beyond what you think are your limits, all with a greater vision of assisting you in what you are trying to achieve.

After these many years, I still remember Robert Ernest and his strong architecture. I also remember his comments on Paul Rudolph being a great mentor — and my experience proved that Robert was right!

—September 2022, Sarasota

Donald Singer

Robert Ernest's limited body of work synthesized space and material into an articulate expression of both life and art. I was in graduate school in 1961 when he designed the house for himself and his family in Atlantic Beach.

Ernest had taken material common to local construction methodology, basically the mundane concrete block, and by leaving the block in its natural, unfinished state and using the block as a module for the shape and dimension of space, created geometry that was unique in its expression of form and use of material.

His work came at the point at which I was forming my own rationale for developing architectural space. I had had the good fortune to work with Charles Reed in Hollywood, Florida, and Ernest's clarity underscored the simplicity that Reed had achieved with masonry.

Later, in my own work, I found the concrete block to represent, directly and with no pretentious intent, both the hand of the workman who put it in place as well as a clear expression of how this "thing" was made, something that, even before I was ready to work with clients, I found myself looking for in building design.

In several ways, Robert Ernest's work, albeit the tragically few examples he completed, clarified all of that for me.

It's now more than sixty years since Bob Ernest built his home in Atlantic Beach, sixty years that have seen developments in high-tech materials and grandiose thoughts regarding housing, and still, the imagery and spatial clarity of Robert Ernest's work make me regret the architecture we missed because of his early departure.

—July 2022, Fort Lauderdale

Bibliography

Robert Griffith Ernest

"Arthur W. Milam House, St. John's County, Fla." *Architectural Record* (November 1962), 126–28.

Dixon, John. *Architectural Design Preview USA*. New York: Reinhold, 1962.

Hochstim, Jan Brooke. *Florida Modern: Residential Architecture 1945-1970*. New York: Rizzoli, 2004.

"In Memoriam: Robert G. Ernest, 1933-1962." *Florida Architect* 12, no. 7 (July 1962).

McCarter, Robert. "Concrete Places in a Landscape of Illusions." *The Architecture of Donald Singer, 1964-1999*. Fort Lauderdale: Bienes Center for the Literary Arts, 1999.

McCarter, Robert. "The Modern is Not a Style: Florida's Other Tradition of Architecture." *In Four Florida Moderns: The Architecture of Alberto Alfonso, René González, Chad Oppenheim, and Guy Peterson*, by Saxon Henry. New York: Norton, 2010.

McCarter, Robert. "Along this New but Ancient Way: Alfred Browning Parker and Modern Architecture in Florida." In *The Architecture of Alfred Browning Parker: Miami's Maverick Modernist*, by Randolph C. Henning. Gainesville: University Press of Florida, 2011.

Mitarachi, Paul, and Robert Ernest. "Mykonos and Patmos." *Perspecta 6: The Yale Architectural Journal* (1960): 79–87.

"P/A Eighth Annual Design Awards." *Progressive Architecture* 42 (1961): 97–156.

Pottinger, Robert. "In Memoriam: Robert Ernest." *Perspecta 9/10: The Yale Architectural Journal* (1965): 8–16.

"Record Houses of 1962," "A Multi-Level House with Service Towers." *Architectural Record* (May 1962): 136–39.

"Record Houses of 1963," "Sculptured House of Concrete Block." *Architectural Record* (May 1963): 70–73.

Stuart, John A. "Review of *Re-Reading Perspecta: The First Fifty Years of the Yale Architectural Journal*, by Robert A. M. Stern, Alan Plattus, and Peggy Deamer." *Journal of the Society of Architectural Historians* 65, no. 3 (2006): 457–58.

Wagner, Walter F. *Houses Architects Design for Themselves*. New York: McGraw-Hill, 1974.

Illustration Credits

Unless otherwise noted below, all illustrations published in this book come from the Robert Griffith Ernest architectural archives.

Robert Faesy: Figs. 3i.1 and 3i.2
Judith Gefter, courtesy of Philip Gefter: Figs. 3.2, 3.3, 3b.8, 3b.9, 3b.10, 3b.11, 3b.12, 3b.13, 3b.14, 3b.15, 3b.16, 3b.17, 3b.18, 3b.20, and 3b.25
Emily Haller: Figs. 3a.16, 3a.16a, 3a.17, 3a.19, 3a.20, 3a.21, 3a.21a, 3j.7, 3j.8, 3j.9, 3j.10, 3j.11, 3j.12, 3j.13, and 3j.16
Library of Congress, courtesy Joseph King: Fig. 3.1
Min Lin: Figs. 3b.1, 3b.2, 3b.3, and 3b.4
John W. Molitor architectural photographs, 1935–1985, Avery Architectural and Fine Arts Library, © Columbia University in the City of New York: Figs. 3a.10, 3a.11, 3a.12, 3a.13, 3a.14, 3a.15, and 3a.24
William Morgan, courtesy of University of Florida Architectural Archives, Special and Area Studies Collection: Fig. 4.2
Jerry Uelsmann, courtesy of Donald Singer: Fig. 4.3

A note on the Robert Griffith Ernest architectural archives:
Following his death in May 1962, Ernest's widow, Lynwood, collected and stored the office sketches, drawings, models, photographs, and documents in Ernest's studio at Atlantic Beach. Some of the models, drawings, and photographs were copied or used as originals in the exhibit *In Memoriam: Robert Ernest* that took place at Yale University's School of Architecture sometime before 1965, organized by Ernest's friend Robert Pottinger (the materials in the exhibit are documented in *Perspecta 9/10*); apparently some of the materials were not returned to Atlantic Beach. Around the time she moved out of the Atlantic Beach house to a smaller apartment in 1993, Lynwood Ernest Dyal kept the smaller archives materials but discarded "a crate of models, numerous drawings, large-scale photoprints from a Yale exhibition, and other materials, all due to her lack of storage space," as stated in the notes from William Morgan to the author on April 11, 1999. After deciding to move to California in 1999, Lynwood Ernest Dyal collected the remaining materials and gave them to Morgan, who in turn gave them to the author for use in this monograph, after which they are to be donated to the University of Florida Architectural Archives in Gainesville, Florida.

Of the original six-page, handwritten catalog of the Robert Ernest archive material that William Morgan made on April 9, 1999, with Lynwood Ernest Dyal, all items remain in the collection with the exception of three dozen 35mm color slides of the Robert Ernest House, six dozen 35mm color slides of the Eli Becker House, and (most critically) one dozen 35mm color slides of the Municipal Youth Center (taken by Robert Pottinger). These may not have been received by Morgan and were not transferred to the author with the rest of the archives. However, the author would appreciate any information on these missing items, as they likely provide invaluable documentation of Ernest's three built works.

Acknowledgments 169

I first became aware of Robert Ernest's three built works in Jacksonville shortly after arriving to the University of Florida as department chair and professor of architecture in the summer of 1991. During a 1992 tour of the Jacksonville and St. Augustine areas with architect, preservationist, and University of Florida professor Herschel Sheppard, we briefly visited the Robert Ernest House in Atlantic Beach. Around the same time, the Jacksonville architect William Morgan (who I had known since he was a visiting professor at the School of Design in Raleigh, North Carolina in 1976), gave me his personal and passionate introduction to Ernest's work, and took me on a tour of the Robert Ernest House in Atlantic Beach and the Eli Becker House in Jacksonville (which Morgan would renovate in 1995–96). During my early years in Florida, I learned of the importance of Ernest's three built works for the work of some of Florida's most renowned architects, including William Morgan, first and foremost, but also Robert Broward, Donald Singer, and Carl Abbott, among others, to all of whom I owe a debt of gratitude for making me aware of Ernest's work and how it had influenced their own work.

In 1999, the surviving archive of Robert Ernest's work was given by his widow, Lynwood Ernest Dyal, to William Morgan, who immediately transferred it to me, with the understanding that I would author a monograph on Ernest's work. (The history of the Robert Ernest archive is presented in a note in the illustration credits of this book). I want to acknowledge my University of Florida colleagues, Professors John Fernandez and Nancy Clark, for their early enthusiasm for Ernest's work, and assistance in "unpacking" the Ernest archive. However, responsibility for the delay in the completing the research and realizing the monograph from 1999 to 2023 must remain entirely my own.

In 2019 my teaching and publishing commitments finally abated enough to allow me to turn my attention to the task of employing the Robert Ernest archives to assemble a monograph on his all-too-brief career in architecture. At that time, I contacted Ernest's older brother Albert Ernest Jr., and his daughters, Kim Brough Ernest and Kristin Markell, who over the last four years have provided essential insights and answered my specific queries on facts and dates, as well as, most importantly for me, being enthusiastic supporters of my efforts to realize a monograph on Ernest's works.

During the last four years, I want to acknowledge the invaluable contributions of my graduate student research assistants at Washington University to this project: Kinga Pabjan, who made a full inventory and documentation of the Ernest archives, as well as assisting in contacting the Ernest family and various other archives; Emily Haller, who built and photographed the models of the Youth Center and Ernest House; Shen Li, who researched archives containing photographs of Ernest buildings, as well as scanning a large portion of the materials from the Robert Ernest archives published in this book; and Min Lin, who built and photographed the model of the Becker House.

I would like to thank Robert A. M. Stern who, in addition to being the former dean of the Yale School of Architecture, was, while an architecture student at Yale, the editor of the 1965 issue of *Perspecta 9/10*, which was dedicated to the memory of Robert Ernest. Stern's remarkably clear memories of the events involved in assembling the *Perspecta 9/10* issue, as well as his sharing of his correspondence with Robert Pottinger, who wrote the piece memorializing Ernest for the issue (and who was rumored to have taken a dozen photographs of the completed Youth Center after Ernest's passing—photographs that have yet to be located), was most helpful to me. I would also like to thank A. Robert Faesy, architect and former student photographer for the Yale School of Architecture, who is credited with talking two model photographs used in Pottinger's piece on Ernest in *Perspecta 9/10*, and who kindly shared his memories.

I would like to thank Philip Gefter for permission to use his mother, Judith Gefter's beautiful photographs of Ernest's Eli Becker House, as well as her photographs of Paul Rudolph's Milam House. I would like to thank Joseph King, coauthor of the comprehensive monograph on Paul Rudolph's Florida houses, for providing the Rudolph perspective of the Milam House, and, more recently, bringing to my attention the 1957 letters from Rudolph to Bert Brosmith, lead associate in Rudolph's Sarasota office, regarding Ernest's summer apprenticeship. I would also like to thank Donald Singer for providing Jerry Uelsmann's beautiful photographic collage of the Ernest House and a vernacular Florida Cracker house that was published as the cover of the *Florida Architect* in 1967. I would like to thank Rina Vecchiola and Jennifer Akins of the Kenneth and Nancy Kranzberg Art and Architecture Library at Washington University for their assistance in assembling the Ernest bibliography. I would like to acknowledge the efforts, sadly unsuccessful, to track down the color slides listed in the Robert Ernest archives catalog, but no longer in the archives, of John Nemmers, associate chair, Special and Area Studies Collection and Architectural Archives, University of Florida George A. Smathers Libraries. Finally, I would like to thank Donald Singer and Carl Abbott for their insightful thoughts on Ernest that are included as the "Afterwords" in this book, and also to thank Kristanna Broward Barnes for permission to reprint Robert Broward's beautiful remembrance of Ernest, first published in 1962, as well as for her generous donation to assist in the publication of this book.

1. This and other personal information regarding Robert Ernest are from my email correspondence and telephone calls, spanning 2018 to 2022, with his older brother, Albert Ernest Jr..

2. One might also notice the blackface jockey statues on either side of the entry walkway, and the Black (or blackface) man playing a banjo on the front stairs, as well as the lack of Black people inside the building—a regrettable but likely accurate reflection of the lack of diversity on campus at the time.

3. Ernest's undergraduate transcript from the University of Virginia, part of the Robert Ernest archives.

4. Perhaps only days after Ernest had departed Rudolph's Cambridge office at the end of the summer of 1955 to return for his fourth year of studies at University of Virginia, William Morgan arrived in the United States after three years in the Navy in the western Pacific and began his graduate studies at Harvard's Graduate School of Design. The first thing Morgan did in the late summer of 1955 was to apply for work at Rudolph's office, where he was employed until the end of 1956; Richard Shieldhouse, *William Morgan: Evolution of an Architect* (Gainesville: University Press of Florida, 2018), 26–35. Morgan would go on to become one of the most important modern architects in Florida, with his practice based in Jacksonville from 1964 to 2016, and he often stated that his work was inspired by the three built works Ernest would realize in Jacksonville from 1959 to 1962. Morgan would be instrumental in assuring the preservation of the Robert Ernest archives, on which this book is largely based (see acknowledgments).

5. In Ernest's portfolio, this competition project is listed as a "3rd year design," made in 1956, but the year and associated classes indicate that this was made during his fourth year.

6. Letters from Paul Rudolph to Bert Brosmith, 2 June 1956 and 17 July 1956, Library of Congress/ Smithsonian; courtesy of Joseph King. King is the coauthor of the definitive book on the early career of Rudolph in Florida: Christopher Domin and Joseph King, *Paul Rudolph: The Florida Houses* (New York: Princeton

Architectural Press, 2002); I am indebted to King for bringing these letters to my attention quite late in the writing of this book.

7. Paul Mitarachi and Robert Ernest, "Mykonos and Patmos," *Perspecta 6: The Yale Architectural Journal* (New Haven: Yale University, 1960), 78–87.

8. As far as I have been able to ascertain from my research into the records of Burk, LeBreton, and Lamantia, Architects, none of Ernest's designs from his internship with the firm—convent, baptistry, fire station, or high school gymnasium—were realized according to his designs.

9. George Kubler, *The Shape of Time* (New Haven, CT: Yale University Press, 1962), 33, 10, 55. See also his encyclopedic *The Art and Architecture of Ancient America* (London: Penguin, 1962).

10. William MacDonald, *The Architecture of the Roman Empire* (New Haven, CT: Yale University Press, 1965) and William MacDonald, *Early Christian and Byzantine Architecture* (New York: George Braziller, 1962).

11. Frank Brown, *Roman Architecture* (New York: George Braziller, 1961).

12. Vincent Scully, *The Earth, the Temple, and the Gods* (New Haven, CT: Yale University Press, 1962).

13. Vincent Scully, *Frank Lloyd Wright* (New York: George Braziller, 1960).

14. Mary Emma Harris, *The Arts at Black Mountain College* (Cambridge, MA: MIT Press, 1987), 17.

15. Josef Albers, 'The Educational Value of Manual Work and Handicraft in Relation to Architecture', in Paul Zucker (ed.), *New Architecture and City Planning: A Symposium* (New York: Philosophical Library, 1944), 688–94.

16. Harris, *The Arts at Black Mountain College*, 17. Albers's teaching at the Bauhaus, Black Mountain College, and Yale has been comprehensively documented and analysed in Frederick A. Horowitz and Brenda Danilowitz, *Josef Albers: To Open Eyes* (London: Phaidon, 2006).

17. Kahn, quoted in Richard Saul Wurman, *What Will Be Has Always Been: The Words of Louis I. Kahn* (New York: Rizzoli, 1986), 244.

18. Riverview High School, Sarasota, Florida, 1957-58, and Sarasota High School, Sarasota, Florida, 1958-60. It should be noted that both buildings were models of what we would today call sustainable design, in that they used deep shading roof

overhangs, external sunshades protecting the operable glazing in the facades, internal chimney-effect assisted through ventilation, and the engagement of prevailing breezes, all to mitigate the hot, humid Florida climate without requiring the use of mechanical air-conditioning.

19. Paul Rudolph, quoted by Allan Greenberg in Robert A. M. Stern and Jimmy Stamp, *Pedagogy and Place: 100 Years of Architectural Education at Yale* (New Haven: Yale University Press, 2016), 176.

20. William Morgan, the Jacksonville architect who has been most closely associated with Robert Ernest's legacy, including renovating Ernest's Becker House in 1995-96 and shepherding Ernest's archives between his widow Lynwood and the author in 1999, is also the architect most closely associated with the documentation and practice of earth architecture, having authored four books on ancient mound-building cultures around the world, as well as his final book, *Earth Architecture: From Ancient to Modern* (Gainesville: University Press of Florida, 2008), which, as its title suggests, traces the tradition of earth architecture up to the present day.

21. Vincent Scully, *Louis I. Kahn* (New York: Braziller, 1962), 25. "The impression becomes inescapable that in Kahn, as once in Wright, architecture began anew. With Kahn, as with Wright, the germinal project was cross-axial in plan. This was the Bath House for the Trenton Jewish Community Center, of 1955-56." Scully's prescient book, written in 1961, when Kahn had built only a handful of projects, shows astonishing critical foresight in predicting the great things that were to come.

22. This type of house plan, with the L-shaped primary spaces wrapping around the service core, was the starting point for Frank Lloyd Wright's Prairie house plans; called the "four-square" plan, Wright used it in his own house in Oak Park of 1886 and in all his subsequent house plans that derived from it.

23. The practicing architects among the readers will perhaps notice the fire egress (means of escape) problem evident in Ernest's apartment plans as drawn, as each apartment only has access to one of the two stair towers that serve the floor, rather than to the two separated means of egress required by code. However, the solution to this problem is already in Ernest's ingenious plan, as the terrace of each apartment touches one of the other pair of stair towers, serving the floors above and below, and a door from the terrace into the stair tower would provide the needed second means of egress.

24. In his sketch of Kahn's housing design, Ernest simplifies it by substituting triangles for the hexagons around the perimeter; whether this was intentional

modification or simply the result of the rush to document the image during the lecture, I leave to the reader.

25. This project, which was included in the pages of the portfolio with the other Yale work, could be a competition entry made around the same time Ernest was at Yale. But there are no notes to that effect in Ernest's portfolio, as there are for the other independent projects not connected to school or a particular office. When including a competition entry in his portfolio, Ernest usually provided a text or caption with the program and other information. If this existed in this case, it has been lost.

26. Ernest's employment with Mann and Harrover in Memphis, as well as his employment with Burk, LaBreton, and Lamantia in New Orleans, known as internships or apprenticeships, were required, along with his receiving a professional degree in architecture (in his case from the University of Virginia), in order for him to take the architectural licensing exam. Today the United States remains one of the few countries in the world that require this apprenticeship or internship period in addition to the professional degree in order to become licensed as an architect.

27. This first project, one of Le Corbusier's most studied designs, was not realized, and Le Corbusier's second realized design for the villa was completely different from the first: a three-story structure with no double-height spaces, the "free-plan" of which was ringed by narrow exterior terraces on all sides. For Le Corbusier there was evidently a mutually exclusive relationship, requiring a choice of one or the other, between the "free-plan" of the second Carthage Villa design, which necessitated the flat floor slabs on which to dispose the free-form walls, and the stepping, interlocking section, with its floors, walls, and ceilings folding into one another (perhaps best named a "free section"), of the first Carthage Villa design.

28. Sharp-eyed observers will note that the perspective shows the version of the west wall of the studio with full-height horizontal wood louvers, which Ernest clearly considered using until quite late in the process.

29. "Citation: Residential," *Progressive Architecture* (January 1961), 132–33.

30. "A Multi-Level House with Service Towers," *Architectural Record* (May 1962), 136–39.

31. Robert Broward, from the July 1962 issue of the *Florida Architect*, dedicated to the memory of Robert Ernest.

32. This three-lobed version of the swimming pool, though erased and replaced with the single-hexagon plan, can still be discerned as faint lines in the final site plan.

33. Ernest initially intended to use the triangular-in-plan-shape concrete blocks he documented in an early drawing. He notes that the triangular blocks, which have three eight-inch-square outer faces and a two-inch-diameter vertical hole at their center, could be made using the same amount of concrete as a standard concrete block (eight-by-eight-by-sixteen inches), but would be much more solid and structurally capable. However, the triangular blocks can only be set in a non-structurally interlocking stack bond, as opposed to the structurally interlocking running bond possible with standard concrete block, as well as with his rhombus-shaped concrete block, and this accounts for his use of the latter in the Eli Becker House.

34. Robert Broward, from July 1962 issue of the *Florida Architect*, dedicated to the memory of Robert Ernest.

35. Robert Pottinger, "In Memoriam: Robert Ernest," *Perspecta 9/10*: The Yale Architectural Journal (New Haven, CT: School of Architecture, Yale University, 1965), 8–6. This issue of *Perspecta*, edited by Robert A. M. Stern, is a record of a discipline in transition, exemplified by its cover with half of the plan of the classical Palace of Charles V in Granada spliced together on the diagonal with half of Louis Kahn's first design for the Rochester Unitarian Church; the selections from Robert Venturi's *Complexity and Contradictions in Architecture*, to be published the following year; to George Kubler's "What Can Historians Do For Architects?" an essay on the engagement of history understood as "the shape of time" in architecture school curricula; and Louis Kahn's laconically titled "Remarks," a meditative consideration of the unprecedented works then emerging from his office, including the national capital at Dhaka, the Indian Institute of Management in Ahmedabad, and the Salk Institute for Biological Studies.

36. This from an interview of A. Robert Faesy with the author on 24 April 2020.

37. It is not clear whether this model of the apartment tower was discarded in the early 1990s along with all the other models in Ernest's archive, but it also does not appear to be in the Yale student work archives.

38. Jimmy Walker, "Seek Bids on $85,000 Youth Center for Sept. Construction," *Jacksonville Journal* (January 1962); total costs included an additional $26,000 for furnishings and equipment.

39. Walter Wagner and Karin Schlegel, eds., *Houses Architects Design for Themselves* (New York: McGraw-Hill, 1974; Jan Hochstim, *Florida Modern: Residential Architecture 1945–1970* (New York: Rizzoli, 2004).

40. When visiting Ernest's Youth Center in the early 2000s with my faculty colleagues and graduate students from the University of Florida, the staff said they enjoyed the ways the space worked when in use by the children and how the ceiling shaped the three spaces of the main room. But they also asked us why the central interior space is so dark both day and night. We said that the architect had not designed the building to be so dark, pointing out the six large clerestory windows in the ceiling above, which were intended to provide generous daylight and sky views to the central room, but that are now dark and lightless due to the new roof addition.

41. As noted in the first chapter, endnote 4. Morgan worked for Rudolph in his Cambridge office during most of his first year of architecture school at the Graduate School of Design at Harvard University.

42. Robert McCarter, *William Morgan: Selected and Current Works* (Mulgrave, Australia: Images Press, 2002).

43. This from email exchanges between the author and Donald Singer, 22 May 2020 and 22 July 2022. Jerry Uelsmann's photographic prints—what he called "post-visualization" experiments—are documented in *Uelsmann: Process and Perception* (Gainesville: University Press of Florida, 1985), *Jerry Uelsmann: Photo Synthesis* (Gainesville: University Press of Florida, 1992), and *Uelsmann: Yosemite* (Gainesville: University Press of Florida, 1996).

This book is dedicated to **William Morgan** (1930-2016),
modern architect of Jacksonville,
disciplinary historian of earth architecture,
consistent champion of the designs of Robert Ernest,
and respectful restorer of the Eli Becker House,
who was the first to introduce me to Ernest's work.

The author and publisher would like to acknowledge and thank the following persons and institutions for their support of the publication of this book:

The Architecture Faculty Development Funds, 2021–22 and 2022–23, Washington University; the Graduate School of Architecture and Urban Design and College of Architecture, Washington University; and Kristanna Broward Barnes

ORO Editions
Publishers of Architecture, Art, and Design
Gordon Goff: Publisher

www.oroeditions.com
info@oroeditions.com

Published by ORO Editions.

Copyright © 2023 Robert McCarter.

Author: Robert McCarter
Book Design: Pablo Mandel
Typesetting: Silvina Synaj
CircularStudio
Project Manager: Jake Anderson

10 9 8 7 6 5 4 3 2 1 First Edition

ISBN: 978-1-954081-43-7

Color Separations and Printing: ORO Group Inc.
Printed in China

ORO Editions makes a continuous effort to minimize the
overall carbon footprint of its publications. As part of this
goal, ORO, in association with Global ReLeaf, arranges
to plant trees to replace those used in the manufacturing
of the paper produced for its books. Global ReLeaf is an
international campaign run by American Forests, one of
the world's oldest nonprofit conservation organizations.
Global ReLeaf is American Forests' education and action
program that helps individuals, organizations, agencies, and
corporations improve the local and global environment by
planting and caring for trees.